Just
Open a
Vein

Edited by
William Brohaugh

Writer's
Digest
Books

Cincinnati, Ohio

Just Open a Vein. Copyright © 1987 by Writer's Digest Books. Printed and bound in the United States of America. All rights reserved. No part of this book may be reproduced in any form or by any electronic or mechanical means including information storage and retrieval systems without permission in writing from the publisher, except by a reviewer, who may quote brief passages in a review. Published by Writer's Digest Books, an imprint of F&W Publications, Inc., 1507 Dana Ave., Cincinnati, Ohio 45207. First edition.

Library of Congress Cataloging-in-Publication Data

Just open a vein.

    1. Authorship. 2. Authors, American—20th century—Biography. I. Brohaugh, William. II. Writer's Digest Books (Firm)
PN149.J87   1987   808'.02   87-18986
ISBN 0-89879-294-0

Design by Joan Jacobus

The following two pages are an extension of this copyright page.

Just Open a Vein honors all writers who take the risk of revealing themselves on paper, and who discover themselves in the process.

My primary thanks must go to the editor who installed the Chronicle section into Writer's Digest: *John Brady, who gave me editing tools that I will use for as close to forever as I can push it. Other editors who contributed to the quality of this volume, by locating or polishing the articles herein, include Rose Adkins, Tom Clark, Sharon Rudd, Kirk Polking, Leon Taylor and Ed Morris.*

Contents

Introduction

Just Open a Vein, the title of this book, derives from a quote by sportswriter Red Smith, who noted that learning to write was easy. "All you do is sit down at a typewriter, and open a vein."

But Smith didn't have a purely anatomical view of the art. He realized the craft involved in writing, as well. "Writing is very much like bricklaying," he said. "You learn to put one brick on top of another and spread the mortar so thick."

Smith, vein-tapper and bricklayer, was an observer, a commentator, a chronicler. And it is here that we move from the title provided by his words to some other titles, because these other titles—working titles for this anthology—help to explain why this volume was created, how it was put together, and what you will expect to find in it.

My original working title for this collection of intimate essays was *The Writer's Digest Chronicles*. Now, mind you, when I say "original working title," I mean that it was the first working title. No originality went into it, since it just picks up the name of a regular column in *Writer's Digest* magazine, the magazine I edit. Each *WD* Chronicle is a first-person narrative, an examination of this vein-tapping, bricklaying craft, and what drives someone to it in the first place. A Chronicle can be serious, hilarious, questioning, answering, bewildered, knowing. Often all at the same time.

We first began our Chronicle section in 1979, though we'd been publishing Chroniclesque articles for years upon years, in the *Digest* itself, and in related publications, such as our annual *Writer's Yearbook*. Richard Rosenthal, president of the company that publishes *WD*, and one-time *WD* editor and publisher, calls such articles "How-Beats-the-Heart-of-the-Writer" pieces ("How Beats" for short).

Dick's phrase was considered as a potential title for this book, and it would have been accurate. There's a lot of heartbeats and heartbeating on these pages.

Another title considered was *Writer's Heart, Writer's Art*. Apropos, in that it considered not only the heartbeating, but also the results of that beating—the writing itself. Besides, there is art in the writing that describes writing found here. I've been asking writers to write about writing for more than a decade now, and it still surprises me how difficult that task is. That so many writers—all those included here—were able to accomplish the task so well pleases me.

The tales included here have been written by a mix of the well known and the unknown. There are bestselling writers, and there are those whose contributions here represent their first sales. These writers warn of pitfalls, give you perspective on the publishing business, and—above all—help you discover that your problems are not only yours, that you share more with your fellow writers than an intriguing profession.

We are all of one entity. We all share a heart. Our veins are connected.

In the pages that follow, then, let's open those veins, test the pulse within with the point of a pen, discover how beats.

We Were All Beginners Once

by Lawrence Block

I admire Larry Block not only as a writer (his novels are entertaining and readable, not to mention well crafted), but also as a success story. He began where we all begin, as a dreamer imagining publication and success. Then he went out and fulfilled that dream, working hard, working consistently, polishing his skills, maintaining as best as possible his confidence.

Larry writes the Fiction column for Writer's Digest, *and in one of those columns, he noted that he has difficulty writing nonfiction. When you read this, you may well wonder how that could be. As Larry himself explained: "These columns of mine aren't fiction or nonfiction. They're letters to friends, the great majority of whom I haven't met and don't know by name, and they have consequently been the easiest writing I've ever done. And why not? What's easier than writing a letter to a friend?"*

It's just such a letter that is the appropriate opening to this collection, which is, in so many ways, a parcel of letters from friends and colleagues to other friends and colleagues.

One of the first things a writer is asked by a new acquaintance is if he has ever had anything published. There was a time when this irked me, until I saw it as a natural enough way of establishing one's professional status or lack thereof. One may be a painter without being hung or a traitor without being hanged; similarly, one may be a writer without being published, but one cannot be a *real* writer, so, er, ahem, *have* you had anything published, Mr. Block?

Indeed I have, I'll assure my new friend. I've been supporting myself with my typewriter ever since college. I've made, certainly, a better living in some years than in others, but I've always scraped by. And as for being published, I was still in college when my first books and stories saw print.

My conversational partner will nod at this, grateful to know he (or even she) is not in the presence of an impostor, a writer *manqué*. Then a sullen glaze will come into his (or possibly her) eyes.

"You read about the struggle writers have to get published. The years of heartbreak. The endless rounds of rejection slips. The poverty, the menial jobs. But you, you never had any of that, did you?"

Didn't I? "Oh, it was all ages ago," I'll say, "back around the time of Columbus's second voyage. So it's really pretty hard to remember."

Hard to remember? It might have been yesterday.

All I wanted during my first year at college was to be published. I'd decided a couple of years earlier that I intended to become a writer. How was one to manage that? By majoring in English, I supposed, and by reading everything I could lay my eyes on, and, finally, by sitting down at the typewriter and actually writing something.

And then submitting it, whatever it might be. Poems, sketches, three- and four-page short stories. I'd blush to recall the adolescent tripe I had the gall to submit for publication, but for the arrogance implicit in such a blush. Publishers, I now know, are forever inundated with unsuitable, amateurish submissions. My efforts were not even outstanding in their unsuitability, in their amateurishness. I'm sure they were examined and rejected and returned in short order, leaving no impression on the poor slush reader's mind once they'd left his hands.

I remember one of those stories. It was about two feral children in a scientific experiment. There's a global war or some comparable calamity and only those two infants survive. So they grow up and mate and have two children, and they call one Cain and the other Abel.

Oh, dear. I was to learn that every magazine gets that story two or three times a week. And even if that weren't the case, what I'd written wasn't a story. It was just a gimmick afloat on a thousand-word ocean.

And where did I send it? *Harper's, The Atlantic, The New Yorker.* Places like that.

Well, what do you want? I was a beginner. I didn't know any better.

In an autobiography, *Call It Experience,* Erskine Caldwell tells of his first sale. The future author of *God's Little Acre* and *Tobacco*

Road had written some earthy stories about poor folks in red-dirt Georgia. He sent them around and got a letter from Maxwell Perkins at *Scribner's Magazine.* Could Caldwell come to New York to discuss two of his stories?

Caldwell rode up on a bus and Perkins took him to lunch, where they talked about everything but the two stories the young Georgian had sent in. Over coffee the editor said: "About those two stories. I'd like to publish them. I thought we might pay you two-fifty for the short one and three-fifty for the longer one."

Caldwell looked unhappy. Perkins asked if something was wrong.

"Well, I suppose it's all right," Caldwell allowed, "but I thought I'd be getting more than six dollars for two stories."

The first money I ever got from a publisher was two dollars from a magazine called *Ranch Romances.* Pines Publications issued *Ranch Romances,* and at the time it was the last survivor of a whole string of western pulps. It was, editorially speaking, a bizarre hybrid, featuring love stories on horseback, as it were.

In the summer of '56 I spent three months working as a mail boy at Pines Publications. When I got back to college, I clipped some newspaper item and sent it to Helen Tono, who was editing *Ranch Romances.* She bought it as a filler and sent me a check for two bucks, along with a note of encouragement. I don't know if she'd have bought it if she hadn't remembered me. Oh, well. It's not what you know, it's who you know. Right?

It was money from a publisher, and that was something. But it wasn't for anything I'd written.

There was something almost schizoid in my attitude, it seems to me. On the one hand, I believed (or thought I believed) that one ought to be prepared to starve for one's art, that a writer's artistic integrity was his most precious possession.

On the other hand, I would have done anything to get published. *Anything.*

It's hard to remember the urgency of my need to see my words in print. I can see now that what a beginner really needs is not to be published but to grow as a writer. The writing I did was valuable to me, but why did I have to send off all my poems and stories?

I suppose the whole process helped me to take myself and my ambitions seriously. Even the rejection slips, tacked neatly to my dorm-room wall, seemed to validate what I was doing. They were visible proof that I was engaged in a process aimed at eventual publication.

If I hadn't been submitting things, if I hadn't been trying to get into print, I'm not sure I'd have kept writing.

The first money I received for writing of my own was seven dollars from a religious magazine. A friend and I wandered into a Bowery mission one night and watched the down-and-outers endure the service so they could get the meal that followed it. I went home and turned the experience into a seven-hundred-word article. "We Found God on the Bowery," I called it, and I told how what began as a lark ended in a conversion experience. "We came to scoff," I wrote, "but we stayed to pray."

That wasn't what happened. Cynical sophomoric wretches that we were, we came to scoff and scoffed our way home. But, as I told you, I would have done anything to get published. I submitted my story to a magazine published by the denomination that sponsored the mission. They bought it, printed it, paid for it.

They even used my title.

While I was working as a mail clerk at Pines Publications, I wrote a story about a wise-guy crook who works at a drugstore and steals from his boss, then moves on to mail fraud. The mood was pretty good, but it didn't really make a story. Back at school, I polished the story and sent it to *Manhunt*.

It came back with a note from the editor. He liked it, but it needed a snapper for an ending. If I could think of something, he'd like to look at it again.

I couldn't believe it. I ran out, bought a copy of *Manhunt*, read every story in it, then rewrote mine with a new ending in which the narrator is hoist on his own petard, investing his ill-gotten gains in what the reader can tell is phony uranium mine stock. It was a hokey notion, and the story came back with another nice note, saying it didn't really work and better luck next time. I wasn't surprised. I hadn't really expected to sell it.

Meanwhile, I had a couple of poems accepted here and there. And I was producing stories regularly for a fiction workshop class. And one day I thought of a way to redo my *Manhunt* story. I had the narrator move up another rung and become a contract killer. I was pretty sure it worked this time, and I sent it off, and the editor bought it.

A hundred bucks. It was months before I got the money, more

months before the magazine was on the stands. I couldn't wait; I wanted the story to be on sale the day after I got the letter of acceptance.

I'm still like that. I want to type THE END, take the last page out of the typewriter, then walk around the corner and see the book on sale in the stores. My publisher seems to be similarly inclined. He has listed books of mine in his catalog before I've gotten any further than the title, has had covers printed before I've finished the manuscript, and gets the book on the shelves in a fraction of the time most publishers take.

A man after my own heart.

You know what? I'm still a beginner. I've written more books than anyone should have to read, yet every time I hold a new book in my hand I get a thrill not unlike the one I received when I picked up a copy of *Manhunt*. I still try new things, and sometimes they're as ill-advised as my Adam-and-Eve story. I still take chances, and sometimes they work and sometimes they don't. On some level, I still look to publication as a form of validation of who I am and what I do.

In *Cup of Gold*, John Steinbeck's first novel, an old sage said something along these lines to the earnest young hero: "You are young, and want the moon to drink from as a cup of gold. Reaching and straining to catch the moon, you may catch a firefly. But if you grow up you will realize that you cannot have the moon, and would not want it if you could. And you will catch no fireflies."

That's paraphrase; I don't have the book at hand, and it was twenty-five years ago that I read it. There's been a lot of water under the bridge since then, or over the dam, or wherever it goes.

A lot of fireflies, too. Aren't they pretty? And don't they cast a lovely light?

section one

"MY GENETIC DISORDER"
Tales of Writing Influences

Where does our fascination with words and storytelling come from? Is it learned, or inherited? There are different sources. Myself, I really can't tell. I know there are writers I credit with influencing me early on: Thornton Wilder, specifically his Our Town *and* The Skin of Our Teeth. *Ray Bradbury, specifically his* Dandelion Wine. *Robert Heinlein, for his sensible five-point checklist for writing success: Write, finish what you write, do not rewrite except to editorial order, put it on the market, keep it on the market until sold.*

But in so many ways I think that Wilder and Bradbury and Heinlein reinforced what was already in me.

I'd like to know how it got in me in the first place. I'd like to be as sure of it as the people who have contributed the tributes included in this section.

My Genetic Disorder
by Julia Wekkin

"Since writing this article, I have given birth to a second son and an unsold novel," Julia Wekkin reports. "Currently I counsel abusive parents and am at work on a second novel."

I wonder for a moment about the potential analogies between Julia's work with abusive parents, the mention of it so neatly sandwiched into the update of her writing life, and the act of "parenting" a novel. Perhaps the most apt connection an inventive writer might draw would be that a parent allowing a child to grow up to be a writer is an intolerable abuse that maybe some government agency should look into.

But allowing a child to follow his or her dream, especially if that dream is also your dream, isn't abuse. It is genetic blessing.

When Mom would take the tuna casserole out of the oven, open the back door, and shout "Hello" instead of "Supper," passersby were puzzled. But I knew she was working. The Philadelphia cab driver who once instructed her to "go to the corner and wait for the light to turn green before crossing, honey" must have sensed the same thing.

I have never been to Philadelphia, but my own neighbors recently asked why I had sent my three-year-old son out to play in his raincoat and galoshes when the sun had been shining all day. Mom would have understood. I was working. After all, it was the rain that had driven my heroine to the cabin, and the soft sound of raindrops had been with me all day as I wrote. But when I got up from my typewriter to check on my son and saw him and his jacketless friends splashing through imaginary puddles, I knew that I had inherited more from my writing mother than her dark eyes and distant look.

When a guest to my home recently opened the door to the linen closet and was nearly killed in an avalanche of balled-up sheets and towels, I blamed my mother. While I admit that I do not recall anyone ever being attacked by anything from one of her closets, it was common knowledge that Mother was not allowed to handle sharp objects or get behind the wheel of a car while in the middle of a writing project. My guest did not know the disease was genetic, but she was aware of my affliction.

"Now I know how you find time to write," she said.

"Actually, it's not finding time to write that I have trouble with," I confessed. "It's finding time to write and still having time left to do everything else that has always been the problem." Perhaps I should have known, but Mother never told me it would be like this.

One day after retreating to my bedroom to write and emerging to find the seasons had changed, but the dirty dishes remained, I complained to my father. It had been less than nine months between the conception and birth of my 7½-pound son, but my twelve-hundred-word picture book was in its fifteenth month and nowhere near delivery.

"How did Mother do it?" I wailed. "Why does everyone have more time than I do?"

"That's funny," he said. "I thought we all had twenty-four hours in a day."

I have taped a reminder to that effect above my typewriter. It helps me to set priorities. Nonetheless, my time problem remains. For even if I had an extra eight hours a day, I would want to spend ten of them writing. And even though I will never feel a compulsion to fold laundry or apologize to houseguests, I am not a totally self-absorbed cave dweller. So, until I am convinced that the world can solve all its problems without me (or at least until my youngest is old enough to master the microwave), my heart and mind may still be at the typewriter, but my body is frequently committed elsewhere. When I get to feeling too schizophrenic, I remember my mother.

In spite of a busy life and buzzing household, my mother wrote. Without the luxury of private work space, a word processor, or blocks of uninterrupted time, she published. As a teenager, I was impressed when she explained that she had gotten the idea for an article explaining evolution to children while she was vacuuming the living room. At the time it had never occurred to me that anyone thought (especially about Darwin) while cleaning. I suddenly developed a new insight into the glassy look she frequently wore while going about household chores. Since that time I have discovered what Mother and other writers have known about the survival of the fittest. In a household where quiet time is all but extinct, there is a definite advantage to switching on my Eureka and shutting out the world as I attempt to work out a writing problem. There are days when I could listen to the garbage disposal for hours.

Although my third-grade autobiography states emphatically that "I do not want to work when I grow up, I want to be a writter (sic)," I do not remember making such a decision. And as much as I have always loved and admired my mother, I certainly do not recall ever wanting to grow up to be just like her. It is simply that my world has always been divided into those who live life and those who prefer to write about it. And ever since I could hold pencil to paper, I have preferred writing about it. Most people measure history by asking, "What were you doing when . . . ?" I mark time by recalling what I was writing when. . . .

My first writing project was in 1956. I was six and the Russians had just invaded Hungary. However, my parents failed to mail my angry letter to Nikita Khrushchev, and I was not invited to visit the Soviet Union. With my political activism in hiatus, I spent the McCarthy era writing happy plays for neighborhood children. While federal marshals integrated Little Rock Central High School, I wrote stories about Jennifer Sue Cuffey under the pen name Pierotte Julliard. When a penciled submission to *Reader's Digest* failed to evoke even a curt rejection (no SASE), I put off for twenty years any further attempts at publication.

While John Glenn was orbiting the earth, I was providing my sister with fifteen-to twenty-page letters detailing the every movement of one brown-eyed boy named Jeffrey Joseph. Kennedy was assassinated and I wrote poetry. During the Great Society I edited my high school *Clarion*. President Johnson sent troops to Vietnam and I interviewed Bucky Badger, the University of Wisconsin mascot.

I met my husband at the University of Wisconsin shortly before the Army Math Research Center was bombed. He had shoulder-length hair and spoke Chinese. When I brought him home, my parents were thrilled. "He writes so well," my mother said.

I was a honeymooner during Watergate but did little writing. (However, my husband published several articles.) After my first child was conceived, I began writing political pieces for pay. As I would tuck my swelling belly under the table and begin pounding away on my typewriter, tiny feet would kick in rhythm. After my baby was born, the sound of the typewriter seemed to soothe him. By the time my son was two years old, he would see me at the typewriter and ask matter-of-factly, "Making words again, Mama?"

For his third birthday he got his own high-mileage Smith-Corona manual. Now his bloodlines show as he announces, "Don't bother me, I need to think," and becomes the third generation to retreat to his bedroom "to write."

Sometimes when I retreat into my own world to write, I wonder if my family would prefer that I was out in the world selling real estate and striving for the million-dollar club. Then I think of my mother. I remember the pride I felt when I was doing research for a college term paper and came across an article she had written. There in *Theology Today,* next to the likes of Paul Tillich, was her piece entitled "The Heresy of Simple Faith." It was a long way from her first confession story, "I Married My Brother." Years later, I stumbled across a laudatory review of a book of her poetry, and I marveled again at how she had found the time to write. The simple fact is that she managed to write by writing. Writing even when she was too tired, too busy, too sick. Writing whenever she was not doing something else. And frequently even then.

Years ago, when my father had finished packing a suitcase for Mom to take to the hospital, he asked if she needed anything else. Cancer had spread through her body, breathing was difficult, and she had use of only one arm, but she indicated she wanted paper and pencil by her side. Two days later she died. I suspect she was working at the time and never even noticed.

Miz Rosa's Story
by Mary Monroe

*Awhile back, we received an intimate, intriguing, but some-
what unfocused piece from a little-published writer then
calling herself Mary Nicholson-Monroe. I expressed interest in working with her to whittle down the piece and give
it focus; she agreed, and she eventually put together the
touching piece you're about to read.*

*We printed the article, and that seemed to be the end
of it.*

But about two years later, one of Writer's Digest's *contributing editors called me. "I've got a perfect profile subject," he said. "She's got a novel coming out, and everybody in the business is excited about it."*

"What's her name?"

"Mary Monroe."

The novel that was then on its way was The Upper
Room—*a tale, it's important to note, that is in many respects also a part of Miz Rosa's story.*

*I wrote the life story of Miz Rosa in the summer of 1959. I was
seven years old.*

Instead of letting me pick cotton alongside my older sister and
brother that year, my mother volunteered me as a babysitter. I had
to look after a senile, old Italian lady. She was the visiting great-
grandmother of one of the wealthy white families that employed my
mother as a housekeeper.

Miz Rosa, as I was instructed to call her, with her mustache
and thick sideburns, resembled an obese Mark Twain in drag. We
stared one another down at our first meeting. I was dark and tiny.
She was enormous and pale and had silver hair. My long kinky hair
was haphazardly twisted into no less than two dozen plaits secured
at the ends by colored ribbons. Wearing the standard attire for my
cultural station, a frayed, handmade flour-sack smock, I was just as
odd-looking to Rosa as she was to me. During the late fifties, black
Southern mothers had a minimum of respect for fashion when it
came to dressing their children, excluding church etiquette.

Miz Rosa was from Atlanta. At 110, she had been an adolescent when slavery ended. During her deepest moments of senility, she convinced herself that she was a young girl again and that I was a slave playmate named Janey her daddy had bought for her as a birthday gift. She had outlived all of her friends, her children, and most of her children's children. Surviving relatives took turns inviting the fractious old belle into their homes for visits that lasted from a couple of weeks to several months. Miz Rosa was like a child in many ways. My main responsibilities included keeping her from wandering off the front porch of her great-granddaughter's house onto the highway and to make sure she kept her clothes on. I earned a dollar a day, paid in empty redeemable pop bottles.

I had a lot in common with Miz Rosa. We both liked sticking out our tongues at passers-by, throwing rocks at moving cars as we sat on the porch, and telling wild stories to one another, each trying to outdo the other. During quieter moments, Miz Rosa sat whispering to herself and I sat on the porch steps writing, fabricating "true stories" about myself. It was Miz Rosa who decided I should write her biography. She insisted that her life—not mine—would be more interesting. Excited and armed with paper, pencils, and erasers, I began to write as she dictated to me that sultry July afternoon. She began, "I was kidnapped from Mars when I was a itty bitty girl."

"I declare—my mama tole me you was Eye-talian! Born in Naples!" I exclaimed. Miz Rosa swatted my jaw with a gnat swatter.

"My kidnappers carried me off to Naples! Now, like I said, *I was kidnapped from Mars when I was a itty bitty girl . . .*" Several days later, she concluded, "My last husband was General Robert E. Lee." I sat on her spacious lap while she perused the manuscript. "Oh, this here is interesting . . . I declare . . . we'll both be famous . . . this is a real interesting piece of writing . . . I declare . . . yes . . . yes."

"Miz Rosa . . . you're holding the manuscript upside down."

". . . um . . . that's how us Martians read. Didn't you know that, girl? You call yourself a writer!" This time she swatted my jaw with the manuscript. She continued scanning, still holding it upside down. After she finally finished it, I stuffed everything into my notebook and sighed triumphantly. I had written the complete biography of a wealthy white woman—and a Martian at that! I was proud of myself. Other than me and Miz Rosa, no one else was aware of my accomplishment. If I shared it with my relatives and friends, they might plagiarize my material and get rich off of it themselves, I thought.

I revised my magnum opus that August until I ended up with 400 cryptic, childishly scrawled pages. While I sat rewriting, Miz

Rosa sat humming, snoring, and babbling incoherently. One afternoon she awoke and asked me what I was doing.

"I'm rewriting our story," I said.

"What story, sugar?"

"Your life story," I turned to look at her over my shoulder. She looked confused.

"I didn't know you was a writer," she said.

The degree of her senility never ceased to amaze me. She would often awaken from a sudden snooze and would have forgotten who I was. It would take me awhile to reestablish my identity and our relationship. During the last week of my babysitting commitment, I was absent from my post for two days. A family illness had kept my mother away from her regular housekeeping duties. When we returned to Miz Rosa's house, I rushed to the old woman's bedroom.

"You, girl—you can't just roam into my room!"

"But it's me, Miz Rosa. Mary." I stood in the doorway of the bedroom clutching my pencils and yellow-lined note pads.

"Mary who?"

I was devastated. This time it took me two hours to refresh the old woman's memory. By the end of the day, she was somewhat coherent.

"I'm going to miss you, Janey," she said.

"Mary," I corrected.

"Where's my Janey?"

I sighed for the hundredth time. "You said she run off to Canada during the Civil War."

"Oh. Then whose little ole girl are you?"

"I'm the Nicholson's little ole girl."

"Oh. You the one what's been helping me piece my life story together?" she asked excitedly.

"Yes, ma'am."

"I'm going to miss you, Mary. They're fixing to ship me back to Atlanta. You've been like a mama to me, I declare, you have." I climbed up on her familiar lap and we embraced one another for the last time. Before I left her that day, she forgot who I was as well as the book we had collaborated on. I went home and gingerly placed the manuscript on top of my bedroom chifforobe and concentrated on other projects.

Later, as a teenager, I spent most of the money I earned picking cotton on postage and writing supplies. I was passionately intrigued by domestic situations and wrote about them exclusively. These stories were usually inspired by watching too many soap operas and reading too many confession magazines. My writing career was yet to get off the ground. My handwritten manuscripts were promptly returned within days after my submissions. The accompanying form letters—usually unsigned and undated—gave me no idea why my stories were being rejected. One editor stamped OBVIOUS REJECTION on the first page of one of my manuscripts.

I was in a fever of desperation. Miz Rosa, who'd comforted me during my first experiences of writer's block, was my last hope. I retrieved my Miz Rosa story from where I had hidden it more than eight years before. After a thorough, objective examination, I realized I had nothing more than a four-hundred-page disaster. The project that had once been so dear to me could be best described as science fiction—let alone a biography! I thanked God that no one but me would ever know of this particular writing folly.

But for some reason or other I was convinced I still had a story somewhere within my four-hundred-page flop. I began to rewrite it again. Within a week, Miz Rosa's biography had been modified extensively. I now had a twenty-page confession story entitled "I Married a Hairy Old Beast." Miz Rosa became Mr. Ross. Like Miz Rosa, Mr. Ross had a mustache and sideburns. And he was old—hence, a hairy old beast. The heroine in the story was a beautiful teenager who had been pressured into marrying a hairy, middle-aged, widowed friend of her father's. In the South, some women marry at an early age. Many of the marriages are literally arranged by the girl's parents. In a lot of the cases I was familiar with, girls were encouraged to marry much older, solvent men. Love and romance were rarely a part of the matrimonial deal. I had many pragmatic cousins who obtained husbands in this manner. The plot of the very first story I was to sell was easily formulated. A minimum of imagination was required in creating the characters. I had known them all, all my life.

When the story was ready to submit, I typed a flowery cover letter on a sheet of perfumed stationery I'd stolen from my older sister. I taped and stapled my package, insured it for two dollars, and sent it by special delivery. I had written my name and address on both the front and the back of the large manila envelope containing the story.

After not hearing from the confession publishing house editor for three excruciatingly slow months, I became depressed. One unusually gloomy day—career day—I dragged myself home from school. My class had had to sit through hours of lectures. Visitors from various career fields had paid their annual visit. During the class discussion, my classmates revealed career plans that included nursing, teaching, the military and even entertainment. I had barely participated in the conversation. I was a failure at fifteen. Finding a tolerable husband I could hide behind seemed like an attractive alternative . . . since no one was ever going to publish me. I'd been born a writer, but destined to fail.

But when I arrived home, I removed an official-looking letter addressed to me, with what was obviously a check peeking out of the window of the envelope, from our roadside mailbox. I gasped as I ripped open the envelope, almost ripping the check in half. *Deliverance*. I fell four times running toward the house and up onto our front porch. I stood in the doorway, waving the $25 check at my apathetic sister and one of our ubiquitous cousins.

"I did it—I finally sold one of my stories!" I exclaimed. My cousin did not even look up from the television. She just belched. My sister half looked up.

"Close that door before you let them flies in here," my sister said.

However, by the end of the day, nine people had requested cash loans ranging from a dime to "a few dollars 'til payday." I look back on that monumental day with great sadness. It was the $25 check everyone was interested in, nothing more. Not a single person asked which magazine my story would appear in, let alone what the story was about.

Even after I purchased twenty copies of the magazine that featured my story, no one was even remotely interested in reading it. My sister stared at the male model in my story's illustration and said: "He sure is cute. You think your editor people could tell you his name and address so you could give it to me?"

I never saw Miz Rosa again. She died the spring of the following year after our association. She would never know how important she had been to my writing. She had been a challenge. She had motivated and inspired me. Her stories had been big. I had had to strive to make mine even bigger. This meant developing my imagination far beyond my previous requirements.

But more important, Miz Rosa helped me develop skills of observation. In one of her rare coherent moments she told me: "Mary, sugar, if you're going to write books about real people, write about people the way they really are. Pay attention to people. The way they act and all. You got sense enough to know that white people and colored people are different in many ways. Kids is different from old folks. A colored kid raised up North by a rich family is bound to be a whole lot different from a colored child like you. If you want people to take you and your stories seriously, give them something that's realistic. Something real people can relate to. Say you was to write you a play and a blind man was to attend it. Just from listening to people talk and what they say tells a person a lot. You don't have to see a person to see his personality. You take this here blind man, he ought to be able to tell the coloreds from the whites, the young from the old and so on."

She hadn't had to say that. Just being with that unusual old woman had taught me that lesson.

Thank you, Miz Rosa.

St. James, Annie, and Me
by Tom Morgan

We write for many reasons. To make money, for one, as Tom Morgan, author of Money Money Money *and writer/ host of the nationally syndicated* Tom Morgan's Moneytalk *radio program, would certainly agree. But we also write to explore, to rediscover, to reveal ourselves not only to our readers, but also to ourselves. And that is something with which Tom Morgan would also readily agree. In fact, he put his agreement in writing. And this is it:*

You're slipping out, then, ducking past the arched brows of the night clerk, at 1 in the A.M., to visit St. James? To pay your respects to an old church?

My sensible side digs its toes in the earth, barks at the slice of writer in me.

It's enough that you allow this church to lure us across Michigan this night for you to reminisce on location. But must you go out at 1 A.M.? You and your church will both be here in the morning! Reunite then.

Ah, but there are more in this tryst than you and St. James, aren't there? Own up. There's Annie! Twenty-five years in your past; surely she's pressed, in wait, to her window this night.

Or if she's not she's pinned a note to her door: If Tommy Morgan ever returns, if he sucks in courage enough to ford the street and tread the walkway to the house, he may note that I married a rug salesman and we moved to Tucumcari, New Mexico, to find work.

Such are my thoughts one evening, or morning, in Bay City, Michigan. I am there, a thousand miles from home, to burrow for the taproot of a novel I wrote. Some might call it a manuscript, without a publisher's imprimatur, in a drawer in my home in upstate New York, a single rejection clipped like a good conduct ribbon to its breast; victim of a schedule that yields no time for its rewriting and pursuit of a publisher.

While you write a novel, it squirms in your every fiber. Its characters jostle you awake with their problems. They hound you with changes they want in their dialogue. Their laughs shatter your somber moments. The settings shift uninvited. Buildings and trees stir within you until they feel comfy.

Your mate grows chary of the moods you bring to breakfast; they vary according to whichever character slept with you.

At least this is how a novel, in the writing of it, moves me. Once written, the novel eases its grip and issues weekend passes for me to explore new stories. And finally, when it is typed and corrected and retyped and submitted, it releases me the way a family does its grown son; I'm expected to visit, but not to stay.

This novel never lets go. I know now it is with me to the end. A few months after I wrote it, I didn't know this. I knew—or thought I knew—that it begged a final chapter, not a written one, but one performed; an essential ritual, a cork punched into that jug of heady wine of the self.

The ritual is to return to the scene, Bay City. The novel is there, twenty-five years ago, when I was a lad in St. James Church and School, in love with a girl named Annie. Half the novel is fiction. The other half is as true as memory can keep it. Blushing Annie is true. Shy Tommy Morgan is painfully true; I know. The church and school and neighborhood are true.

So, returning to New York from Chicago, I make the pilgrimage. I arrive at the city's Holiday Inn at 1 A.M., an August Saturday morning in 1978, but it is no time to bed down. The hour and my sensible side notwithstanding, the church and school and other memories beckon.

Now don't be disappointed if something is gone. A lot can happen in twenty-five years. You've got to expect change. I tell myself this as I hurry up a broad street toward Columbus Avenue and pass Ray's Food Fair, which looks unchanged, down to the red neon sign, from the time when I slouched in our '49 Ford while my parents lugged out a week's groceries for five of us for twenty bucks and muttered how food prices were out of sight.

Columbus Avenue. We all lived on Columbus—St. James, Annie, and me. This is the lower part. I don't recognize a building. Maybe it's not the lower part after all. Maybe the old church is gone. It can't be. I jog up the avenue to a corner where I can make out its dull silhouette. I jog another half block and stop, my breath the only sound. I shiver. There, a sphinx in the night, is St. James Church.

It's grimier than I recall. Its steeple looms taller, steps seem smaller. Its doors give not a mite, and I hear a nun boast that God's church never locks its doors. But that was God and church and nun and boast of a quarter century ago.

Oh to be twelve again and within, enthralled with the High Mass choir and organ that throbbed, to a lad, like the generous heart of all Christendom. To bear my burst of flowers to the communion rail to be thrust into the altar's blaze of color of the May procession.

Tomorrow. I will come here tomorrow. Maybe there will be a Mass. Though I'm not of the faith now, and my words in the novel rebuke the church as an institution of that period, I will return tomorrow, like the critical son to his mother's deathbed. A poor analogy. Mother church has no more than arthritis.

Down the flank of the church, the route we marched mornings from Mass to class. I hear the chatter of the wooden beads that swing from sister's waist.

The convent. Unchanged. Uneasiness here, for my only visit to it was with my father, for him to hear of my despicable behavior lately in school.

Is it still home to two dozen nuns? I doubt it. There are few convents left that shelter that many. Rare is the Catholic school that vaunts four nuns these days.

The gym. Something of a brick Quonset hut. Was I the only boy who ever flung the ball at the wrong basket here? Drafty home of parish fairs and Knights of Columbus breakfasts that followed Masses, in which the Knights clanked down the aisle, plumed hats pressed to their breasts, sabers aglitter in wait of the heavenly moment when they would pierce the black hearts of infidels in defense of St. James and all Christendom. The sabers, I mean. The Knights, I suspect, trooped there to partake of the pleasures of breakfast and conviviality.

And beyond the corner of the gym, the school. But where is the school? There is not a trace of it, only an asphalt parking lot for the new high school. The new high school was under construction in my last year at St. James, the seventh grade. And Christ in the flesh at the blackboard could not have vied with the mortal who flung white hot rivets into the air and the man, three stories up, who snared them, clunk, with tin funnel and flailed them into the beam, around which his legs were curled. Our prayers were for wretched Chinese tots and Pope Pius, and silently for the rivets, that one might plop down the man's shirt front.

Bricks. We were cast into spells by courses of bricks, slap, scrape, plop, tap tap; a check with the level, two more taps; next brick and a new curl of mortar.

Standing in for my old school is a new grade school across the street. It earns only a glance, penance for being there fewer than twenty-five years.

I make my way toward Columbus Avenue again. A pause at the asphalt, in memory of what was there, a tall, red brick school whose wood stairways groaned and whose landings yawned to corral a flock of charges stirring for the bell. A factory of sorts where habited workers fashioned a procession of acolytes, their minds girded with Baltimore Catechism to fend the sins of the world. For insurance, their bodies were adorned with scapulars and Virgin Mary medals, holy cards tucked like inspection notices in their pockets, ashes smudged yearly on their foreheads, nostrils incensed, fingers dipped and shirt fronts and brows dampened with holy water.

Ah, here's the rectory. It is old, substantial, and probably would be imposing if not for its destiny to squat in the shadows of the church that flanks it. To me, there was never another rectory. From A. J. Cronin's to Edwin O'Connor's novels, and lots of others between, there's not a rectory, presbytery, or parish house that doesn't bear resemblance for me to this St. James rectory.

Another lengthy gaze at the church. It is the fount of funds for the other structures, for even the asphalt. It is the haven of faith that bonded all this together, the sanctifier of all the activities on the block, including whatever injustices I felt were perpetrated upon my body and soul in classrooms; the spiritual library of a million confessions forever secret, of mine of boyish sins pursued and expunged by tearful penances of Hail Marys and Our Fathers; monolithic witness of my awe for the host thrust heavenward by priests who, while not bona fide saints, were of sufficient holiness that we scrambled to attention when they appeared at our classroom door. Sanctuary of hosts that seared in blood, for eternity, the pockets of curious boys who coughed them into handkerchiefs—or so we, wide-eyed, were assured.

The reality of it all overwhelms me on this corner of Columbus Avenue. My mind is anointed with memories of these buildings. I have drawn from them to re-create the images in words for my readers. And now to see this, to know for certain that what my twelve-year-old mind preserved for my thirty-seven-year-old mind, indeed exists, stolid in the night, solemn against scudding clouds.

Reluctantly I turn my back on St. James and start up Columbus toward my old home and Annie's. The bakery! Surely not. Classroom breakfast was dispatched from here for every first Friday communicant, a bottle of milk and two slabs of dough, plump with lemon cream and smeared with icing.

There's the City Dairy, Cash n' Carry, ringside to a lunchtime brawl, for which all the boys were thrashed by our nun in the cloakroom.

Past taverns, houses, and stores, some of which I remember, some I'm sure I should recall but cannot.

There is a neon and stainless steel convenience store, flush against our house. To build it, they must have knocked down Bobby Berner's shingled house. He was, as far as I was concerned, the world's only Jewish boy, who consequently did not celebrate Christmas, but saved face one Yule by vowing he'd received a flashlight.

Across the lawns of Bay City Central, beneath the brick face of its stadium, arena of Friday-night miracles against Flint Northern and Bay City Handy and Saturday morning heroics by neighborhood ragtags.

I prop myself against a tree and take in Annie's house, opposite the stadium. Two-storied, narrow, it hugs a strip of land and clutches a small porch to one of its front corners. I was so shy as a boy, so self-conscious as one who buried my lips in Annie's on my pillow, in the dark, where my skinny biceps played proxy. Every minute I look at the house is sixty seconds longer than I managed then, before I dropped my eyes, as I did every morning at St. James with equal reverence for the host.

Where are you now, Annie? And do you ever think of me? Did you ever? It's me, Tom, forever infatuated with your blush, your ivory skin, and lowered eyes. Do you know I never saw your eyes? They were always tucked into your cheeks. They might have been yellow for all I saw. I guess I remain infatuated, in this real and sometimes sordid adult world, with the purity of those days, you bedecked in white layers for our May procession. Where are you now, Annie? Are you alive?

I steal away. The sober side of me chastises my sentimental side for nursing this pointless petal love that flowered twenty-five summers ago. Sentiment's only retort is a smug, if not too confident, "But it's so damned pleasant." You can wing back to blossoms past, and skim over the weeds.

By the hour I reach the church again, the sober side has won out and holds its own in my final inspection of things St. Jamesian from across the street. You old bastard. Solid as, as, the faith of my seventh-grade nun. I trace my steps to the Holiday Inn, moments

before a thunderstorm breaks.

Next morning I discover the name of a classmate—another Tom—in the phone book, and call him. Of course I remember you, he cries. How could I forget? And all that.

He invites me to his suburban house for the afternoon, but before he does, he says, "Funny thing you called this morning. They're just putting the fire out at old St. James Church. Hit by lightning last night. Just the roof, I guess. It's been on the radio."

And he says: "Annie? I think she lives in her old house. Yeah, on Columbus. She's married. Got a couple of kids anyway. I think they go to St. James even."

Within fifteen minutes, my feet sound down the center aisle of St. James for the first time in a quarter century. Something else strikes the aisle for the first time since the structure was blessed and opened to the Irish and Polish immigrants who paid for it: pure sunlight, through jagged gashes in the roof. I see blue sky in puddles on the floor, a floor snaked with hoses and strewn with charred shreds of the roof. Soot spatters the pews.

I approach two young priests and tell them I've not been here for twenty-five years until last night; just before this happened. One shrugs and raises his eyes again to the holes in the roof. The other says, "You live near Binghamton, New York? Father McPhee from Binghamton without the p. In Seminary with him. That's how he introduced himself."

I reminisce for them. I sat just there, twenty-five years ago, every morning, every Sunday. Probably that very pew. And for High Masses, over there with the choir. Father Wynn was here then. And Father O'Brien. They must be dead now.

They are not impressed.

Maybe I should shout: "Hey, dammit! I left here a quarter century ago. Last year I wrote a novel, in large part about this church. It was a damning book, an indictment, if you want to be prosaic. Last night, and not till last night, do I finally visit this church again and half an hour later, ZAP! God's lightning. I'll drop to my knees here, if you will climb into that pulpit and scatter a few blessings and say something reassuring or comforting about this. That's your job, isn't it? Help me understand this. Tell me this is just one colossal coincidence!"

If St. James was there for seventy years, it had a life of 600,000 hours. My visit before the storm was in its final hour. I was probably the last person to see St. James church alive. They never fixed its roof, never reopened it, never proffered another Mass there. Tore it

down and threw up a new one. Little Tommy Morgan drove from Chicago to gaze upon old St. James on its deathbed half an hour before it gave up the Holy Ghost. If he had left Chicago half an hour later, he might have witnessed the lightning, might have called the firemen, might have saved St. James.

Shaken, I stroll up Columbus, buy some filled doughnuts at the bakery, more for nostalgia than hunger. In our old neighborhood, I ask people if they remember my family or those of my pals of the time. Nobody does, except one old man who recalls the Berners. "Jewish folks," he says. "You're not Jewish, are you? They had a fat kid. He's a doctor now. Doing OK." I picture him in white. He peers down a patient's throat, aiming his Christmas flashlight at the tonsils.

To Annie's. With a tightness in my chest, I rap on her door and there she is. For the first time, I see she has eyes! They are squinting, cheery eyes, squeezed above plump cheeks and a broad smile of ample white teeth. Her skin is clear, her figure generous. She is motherly, in charge, a nothing-ruffles-me woman, with a manner as warm as mother's milk.

"You were my first love," she laughs. But in the laugh I detect a tinge of something more than gaiety. Maybe it's only my wishful imagination.

"You never told me."

"Lord! I never spoke to you."

"Nor me to you."

"We were both so shy. It was terrible, wasn't it? I never spoke to a boy until I was a sophomore. Can you imagine it?"

"I wrote a book about you."

"Pornographic?" She smiles always, yet there is even more smile pressing to escape.

"Seriously. About you and me and old St. James. Don't worry. We're both in character. We never say a word to each other."

She laughs. "It'll never sell. Did you hear about the fire?"

"I was there half an hour before the lightning. It was originally scheduled for 1960, but God held off all these years until I showed up again."

"Don't be sacrilegious. I love old St. James."

We chat for an hour and say exactly the sort of things you would. Her husband, reticent, small, and she says moody, leans for a long while against the front door jamb, arms folded, watching kids stream into the stadium across the street for a rock concert. The couple's children, two boys, are not to be seen.

Annie digs out a yearbook and takes me through it page by page. Many of the class I don't recall. Several came after I left, from the eighth grade on. She slips one photo at a time to me of those with whom she graduated. Their best wishes cover the backs, penned in that Palmer style the nuns rapped into our knuckles.

On one of her classmate's photos the farewell message is nothing more than "Remember Tom Morgan?"

"Now why would she write that? This was five years after I left St. James."

Annie shrugs. Her tongue flirts with her lips. Her eyes ease shut for a second and when they open seem to focus somewhere beyond the photo. Altogether, hers is a wistful expression. It's the only answer she offers my question.

Her husband sits in the kitchen when we say goodbye on the front porch. I promise to try to come to the next reunion. She pledges they will look me up if they come camping in New York State. I repeat how wonderful it is to see her and peck her cheek and babble words that half a minute later I forget, for she steadies those squinting mellifluous eyes on mine and as I prattle she deepens her smile and eases her arms to her waist and says, directs, speaks across those twenty-five years and all the pages of that novel, says low in a roguish voice that implies I can cease to babble any time, says with those eyes and that smile and her white hands, her breath, and her voice . . .

"Give me a kiss."

The Man on Stilts
by Candice F. Ransom

The best teachers, whether of writing or of any other skill, instill in their students not instructions and rules and methods, though those can be an important part of the teaching. I look back at those who have taught me over the years, and I see they have taught me attitude. They have taught me love. They have taught me professionalism.

But I never realized the most important of their teachings until I read Candice Ransom's reminiscence about her most influential teacher. Those teachers taught me, as Candice's stepfather taught her, that seeing involves more than simply opening one's eyes.

He came down the dusty road, impossibly long-legged, tall enough to touch telephone wires. Around him, ox-eye daisies drooped in the late September heat and pumpkins lolled in the cornfields like fallen harvest moons.

The boy watched the man's jerky progress, one thumb hooked through the strap of his patched overalls. Strangers seldom came this way. The boy's grandfather claimed he had once seen General Tom Thumb when Barnum's Expedition dazzled the hamlet of Centreville shortly before the War of Northern Aggression, nearly eighty years before. Still, Pap had never mentioned anything about giants.

As the man drew closer, the boy saw his secret. Stilts! He walked on stilts that lifted him three feet off the ground.

"Is that hard to do?" the boy called.

"Not if you want to make a buck." A placard hung around the stranger's neck, extolling the virtues of Little Tavern hamburgers.

"You walk all the way from Washington?" the boy marveled. He had never been to the nation's capital. His father had worked downtown as a trolley car conductor but that was before the Great Trouble that shadowed the land. His father had been out of work now for months, and the boy had abandoned his dreams of ever seeing the magical domes and spires of the District of Columbia.

"Where you headin'?" the boy asked as the stranger passed.

"Don't know." There was a lot of that going around, it seemed.

Aimlessness had become a national disease.

"Could I do that?"

"Try it. Great way to see the world." With a jaunty wave, the man on stilts stalked down the road.

The boy watched the shrinking figure, until the fields turned wine-dark, with only hints of remembered amber.

My stepfather was that boy. And, of all his stories about the Depression, I like best the one about the man on stilts. Times were difficult for my stepfather's family—his descriptions of those days are peppered with accounts of lard-biscuit lunches carried to school in a molasses pail and short-term jobs that involved walking nine miles each way for ten-cent wages.

After the stranger left, my stepfather made himself a pair of stilts and stumbled through the orchards, struggling to master the art of walking with wooden sticks. He slipped off hundreds of times and his father, temper quickened by bad times, busted the stilts into kindling. But my stepfather, fired by some inner desire to see the world from rarefied heights, made another pair. He staggered through the orchards where yellowjackets hovered over ripening peaches and green apples sagged from bowed branches, his perception changed, the dreary days altered by his new sight.

Years later, when he traded his stilts for a ready-made family, he lifted me, a skinny, nondescript kid, up to his special stilt-high perspective, much the way his clumsy stilts had raised him above the dingy moonscape of his own childhood.

I tagged behind him while he did his chores, yet he was never too busy for me. Autumn was brush-thinning time. My stepfather swung the ax and I perched on a log, huge as a felled brontosaurus, scribbling stories in my notebook. When we both got tired, he would tell me the difference between a red oak and a white oak. Once he stopped to heft a rotted log. Underneath were two leopard-spotted slugs, big as puppies.

During spring plowing, I clung to the seat of his old Ford tractor, half-leaning against the chipped fender and half-resting against my stepfather's shoulder. From that noble chariot, he showed me how to read the clouds. Occasionally, the plow blades turned up a white quartz arrowhead, glittering against the red earth like the Hope Diamond. On each pass around the garden, I longed to grab my notebook to write down each new discovery.

I learned to see a peach as it really was—the essence of August contained within a dawn-tinted, velvety globe. The blunted ends of cut cornshocks reminded me of circus tent pegs driven into the ground. Golden gourds lying curled among tangles of morning-glory vines were like secrets waiting to be passed on to the slumbering pumpkins.

I graduated from notebook-scribbling to writing for a living, concentrating my efforts on fiction for children and teenagers.

When my editor asked me to try a historical novel for young adults, I quaked with uncertainty. What did I know about traveling the Oregon Trail in 1846? I had never been any farther west than Kentucky, and an on-site research trip was out of the question. A three-month stint in libraries provided a factual framework for my book, but I couldn't elevate my characters above the black-and-white landscape I had created. They limped through the story. Their actions and motivations lay flat and lifeless on the pages, as if my chapters had been sprayed with the same gray wash that colored the sky during the Depression.

Then, just as the giant once freed a little boy from the tedium of poverty, my stepfather arrived on his homemade stilts to rescue my story. Slumped over my typewriter, I held an imaginary conversation with him.

"How do I know what the trail *looks* like?" I said in despair. "I've never *been* out West."

"So?" My stepfather hobbled around my office. "I'd never been to Washington either. But that didn't stop me from picturing Lincoln in his great stone chair or the towering majesty of the Washington Monument . . . I saw those things because suddenly I believed I *could*. You can, too."

My anxiety eased somewhat. "Will you come with me?" I asked. And so a man on stilts accompanied my fictional wagon train.

Right away he pointed out the necessity to give my heroine a sense of family history. Tying Amanda to a heritage she left behind engaged reader sympathy from the onset and made the enormity of her journey more pronounced. From my stepfather's stilts I saw an ordinary trunk become a precious Pennsylvania Dutch wedding chest. When it is left behind in the dust, Amanda realizes how truly homeless she is, trapped between the known and the unknown. She feels the loss of cholera-stricken friends, not through the pathetic trailside grave crosses, but through the sight of a sweetbriar cutting, which had been carefully nurtured across the plains, angrily tossed away to wither in the sun. My stepfather remarked that the smaller, more specific incident would have more impact than the passive line of graves.

With my stepfather's guidance, I was able to write descriptions that brought vague images into sharp focus: "The plains curved to the horizon in all directions, with the sun beating down, making them feel as though they were traveling in the bottom of a bowl. The sun flattened the life out of Amanda, filled her eyes with the color of blood, made her feel baked to the bone, her skin as taut as a crudely stitched leather moccasin."

I nearly faltered when I came to the Snake River portion of the trail—vaulting bluffs and deep-channeled gorges through which the Snake River writhed—country alien to eyes accustomed to the gentle slopes of the Blue Ridge Mountains.

"Suppose you sent Amanda down the cliff," my stepfather suggested, teetering on his stilts. "Imagine what she'd see, how she'd feel. Don't just describe the scenery, put her in it."

I hesitated. Having my heroine scale a hundred-foot gorge was as foolish as striding the Oregon Trail on stilts. Yet my stepfather was right: this was dramatic territory; it called for dramatic action. I sent Amanda down into the canyon to get water: "With a strange weightless feeling, as though her stomach were floating, she let go of the brush, digging her fingers into the rockface as she inched her way down. . . . Her fingers were cramped into claws, every nail broken to the quick. After a few moments she dared to look up. The top of the cliff soared above her. . . . Beyond the ragged line of stone, the sky unfurled an endless blue banner. Blue sky. Blue water. . . . The world seemed reversed somehow. Which way should she climb?"

Like Amanda, I looked to the sky and earth throughout my novel, aided by the keen perception my stepfather helped me to develop. In subsequent historical books for teens, I employed the same technique, striving to make my heroines' observations heartland-true, and allowing my characters to follow their various paths as accurately as geese vee southward in the fall.

But even as I write about subjects as diverse as the American Revolution and the sinking of the *Titanic*, I am already taking notes for a book, this one featuring a young boy in overalls, standing in an orchard and watching a giant coming toward him.

Going back in time is much easier with my stepfather's legacy. By highlighting details as rich and purple as clusters of pokeberries dangling over a stone wall, my characters transcend the centuries; their struggles and problems become sharp as star-pointed sweet gum leaves. Their stories, patient as pumpkins dreaming in the sun, wait for me to write them down. All I have to do is open my eyes.

The man on stilts was right. It's a great way to view the world.

Ray Bradbury's Children
by Timothy Perrin

When Tim Perrin delivered the profile of Ray Bradbury we had assigned him to write, he wrote in his cover letter, "Please like this. It's the best thing I've ever written."

That would have been a boast had it not been true. And what Tim was recognizing in his piece was not the way he had written it, but the why of the way he had written it. It was a piece of writing celebrating how he had come to writing in the first place.

At Writer's Digest, we publish few profiles that openly place the subject on a pedestal, which this article clearly and unabashedly does. But in this case I had a feeling that WD readers would respect the pedestal, welcome it even, because of how Ray Bradbury's writing must have touched them at some point in their careers. I had that feeling, I admit, because I knew how Bradbury's writing—particularly the exhilarating Dandelion Wine—had touched me. The letters we received after publishing this in our February 1986 issue proved that my feeling was right.

Something else had proven that to me long before we went to press with that issue, though. It's a story I often tell, so bear with me if you've heard it before:

When Tim submitted the story to us, he also sent a copy to Bradbury. Bradbury, who was about to write an original article for us, called me soon after. "Have you read this article?" he asked me.

"Yes."

"What did you think of it?"

"I liked it very much."

"So did I. Why don't you run this instead of something written by me?"

"Actually, I don't see much problem in running both," I said.

"Oh, OK, then. I just didn't want to get in the way of this young writer."

Mr. Bradbury, I am now even prouder to claim that I, too, am one of your children.

Ray Bradbury is a wimp. That's not my word; it's his. I called him a nerd. It went like this:

Q: If I can use the term, I have the feeling you were a nerd.

A: [Laughs.] A wimp.

He's sixty-six years old, wears glasses as thick as Mr. T's forearm, needs to lose thirty pounds, and admits to hating pain, being poor at sports, and being a favorite target of bullies in his childhood. He has lived more than fifty years in Los Angeles, where they build drive-in *churches*, for heaven's sake, and he can't drive. He sent entire cities to Mars more than twenty years before man took his first steps on the moon, yet will spend four days on a train rather than fly to New York.

In other words, a wimp.

So why, I thought, am I sitting in his office crying?

Perhaps it was because this is also the man who put the words in the mouth of Captain Ahab; who turned his hometown of Waukegan, Illinois, into "Green Town" and then transplanted it to Mars; who wrote so well even in his twenties that editors would tell him, "This story is too good for my magazine. I'm going to send it to *Collier's* or *The New Yorker* for you"; who created a family of vampires, fairies, and astral travelers in our midst, then set them wandering on a summer's evening; who brought us an illustrated man with tattoos that move, countless Martians, a twelve-year-old boy with a birth certificate proving he was forty-three, the Rocket Man, firemen who started fires rather than put them out, and a parrot who had memorized Hemingway's last, unwritten manuscript.

Mostly, though, I was crying because this is the man to whom I owe much of what I value in my life, the man who showed me what magic a writer could weave, what universes I could create. This is the man who gave me reasons to want to be a writer and I am crying because I can finally thank him for all that I owe him.

And *he* owes it all to Mr. Electrico.

The Labor Day weekend of 1932, when Bradbury was twelve, the Dill Brothers Combined Shows set up their tents on the outskirts of Waukegan. Mr. Electrico sat in a huge chair, his hair on end, his body glowing with "ten billion volts of pure blue, sizzling power." With a charged sword, he reached out and touched the boy Bradbury on both shoulders, then on the tip of his nose. "Live forever!" he cried.

The next day, on a pretense, young Ray came back and met Mr. Electrico in his uncharged state. A defrocked Presbyterian minister from Cairo, Illinois, Mr. Electrico showed Bradbury the mysteries of the carnival, introducing him to the strong man, the acrobats, the fat woman. Then he told the boy: "We've met before. You were my best friend in France and you died in my arms in the battle of the Ardennes forest. And here you are, born again, in a new body, with a new name. Welcome back!"

That was the stimulus Bradbury needed. He started writing. He wrote tales styled after those he read in *Amazing Stories,* yarns like "The World of Giant Ants." "It was horrible stuff," he says now. He ought to know. He still has all of those stories. He rarely throws anything away.

Then he discovered Jules Verne, H.G. Wells, and Edgar Allan Poe. He read everything by them he could find.

He read just about everything else he could find, too. In 1938, at the tail end of the Depression, he finished high school. But his family was on relief, so college was out of the question. "We had nothing. Nothing except the library, which was everything. I educated myself in the library by going there three, four times a week from the time I was eighteen until I was twenty-eight. I read everything. I went through all the short stories of all the major countries. I read all the major writers in the short story fields. I read all the major plays. I read all the major poetry. It doesn't take that much time. Two hours a day for ten years and you have read everything. Some of it you've read six or seven times."

And he kept writing. Every day. Getting better. "I began to get really good after ten years. I started when I was twelve and when I was twenty-two I wrote a short story called 'The Lake.' It was about a real little girl I knew when I was eight or nine years old. She went into the lake and she never came out.

"That stayed in my mind until I was twenty-two and then I remembered. When I finished that story, I burst into tears and I knew that I had turned a corner in my life, that I had dredged up something. From that time on, I began to go deeper and deeper and deeper. All of the good, weird stories I've written are based on things I've dredged out of my subconscious. That's the real stuff. Everything else is fake."

Bradbury has been dredging like a harbor commission ever since. Anyone who claims to have read everything by him probably doesn't know about half of it. There are the novels. *The Martian Chronicles* is really a collection of short stories. *Fahrenheit 451* took nine days for the first draft. *Dandelion Wine* is a trip back to Bradbury's childhood in Waukegan. His latest, *Death Is a Lonely Business,* is a hard-boiled murder mystery about twenty years in the making ("I had to wait for the characters to come to me one at a time and ask to be in the book"). Then there are the short stories, hundreds of them. There are the Mars stories, the Green Town stories, the Irish stories, the Mexican stories, and all those that don't fit into any category. For years he wrote one a week: first draft on Monday, final draft on Saturday, Sunday to refresh the muse. There are the screenplays: *Moby Dick* (John Huston directed Gregory Peck as Ahab and Bradbury earned an Academy Award nomination), *It Came From Outer Space, The Beast From 20,000 Fathoms,* episodes of the original *Alfred Hitchcock Presents* and episodes of the revival of *The Twilight Zone,* adaptations of his own stories for HBO, and many others. There are the radio plays, the stage plays, the poetry, the essays, and even an opera ("*Leviathan 99*—Moby Dick in outer space").

He writes first thing in the morning, just after waking. "I don't need an alarm clock. My ideas wake me." Characters come and speak to him, like the fire chief from *Fahrenheit 451* who came to Bradbury one morning recently and said, "You never asked me why I burned books."

"You're right," said Bradbury. "I never did ask. Why *do* you burn books?"

The fire chief told him and he added a scene to a novel he originally wrote more than thirty years ago.

"Before I go to sleep at night, I may think of what I might be doing the next day, but the important time is the waking-up time, when you are in and out of the subconscious. You pose questions and they are answered in that half-dream state.

"When I was finishing my new novel, I put myself on that kind of emotional routine. I made a conscious effort to think about the novel before I went to sleep so that my subconscious would give me answers when I woke up. Then, when I was lying in bed in the morning, I would say: 'What was it that I was working on yesterday in the novel? What is the emotional problem today?' I wait for myself to get into an emotional state, not an intellectual state, then jump up and write it." Revision, polish can come later. Now, he wants the guts.

"The trouble with a lot of people who try to write is they intellectualize about it. That comes after. The intellect is given to us by God to test things once they're done, not to worry about things ahead of time."

Bradbury learned to be relaxed about his work when he was in his early twenties and working as a street newspaper vendor for the old Los Angeles *Herald-Express.* "I did it three or four hours a day for about ten dollars a week. When I started, I was yelling, 'Paper! Paper!' After about six months I was getting hoarse screaming the name of the goddamn paper. I experimented one day not yelling to see if it made any difference in the sales. There was no difference. I'd been yelling for nothing.

"That gave me my primary lesson. Don't worry about things. Don't push. Just do your work and you'll survive. The important thing is to have a ball, to be joyful, to be loving, and to be explosive. Out of that comes everything and you grow. All you should worry about is whether you're doing it every day and whether you're having fun with it. If you're not having fun, find the reason. You may be doing something you shouldn't be doing."

If the writing is going well, Bradbury may stay at the typewriter in his basement office at home until he has completed several thousand words. Or he may take the morning's work to his office in what has to be the last antediluvian building in downtown Beverly Hills, just a block from the ultra-chic shops of Rodeo Drive and a few doors up from the Ferrari dealer who sidelines in kiddie-sized sports cars.

His office is cluttered. If he were still a child, his mother would keep him in until he cleaned it. There are manuscripts, mementos, and just plain junk everywhere. A six-foot-tall pink stuffed Bullwinkle J. Moose graces a chair. A painting of Mr. Electrico covers one wall. He has autographed pictures of stars from when he used to hang around the gates of the studios during the thirties— Jean Harlow, George Burns, Gracie Allen. There's a picture of the U.S. pavilion at the 1964 New York World's Fair, which Bradbury helped design. And on the wall behind the couch is a poster-sized picture of Bradbury at the age of three. He has added a comic strip speech bubble that has the boy saying, "I remember you . . . I remember you. . . ."

Bradbury does remember, too. Everything. "I remember being born. I remember having nightmares in my crib. I remember being suckled. I'm very fortunate in this way. But a lot of other people have this information, too. It's never lost. The more you write, the more you word-associate, the more it rises to the surface. After awhile, you are dragging this series of word associations out and you're not sure that you really remember these things, but you do."

Confirmation of his memories came on a trip back home to Waukegan. He bumped into the town barber, a man who had boarded in the home of Bradbury's grandparents in the summer of

1923, the summer of that picture on his office wall. "Your grand-dad had a wine press in the basement," he told Bradbury. "He'd send you and your brother across the street with gunnysacks and you'd come back loaded with dandelions. You'd take them down to the basement and your grandfather would put them in the press and make dandelion wine."

Dandelion wine. Until that moment, Bradbury had not known if he had just dreamed of making dandelion wine or if those memories had been real. "I wrote the book without knowing if it ever really happened, whether I was making it up or not. Here was the town barber telling me fifty years later that it really happened!"

Today an unopened bottle of dandelion wine sits on the corner of Bradbury's desk.

Bradbury says the key to being a writer is not so much talent as rehearsal. "The gift is part; it's there, but you have to rehearse it for many years. Doctors don't suddenly become doctors overnight. They have something in there that comes out for some of them but it takes ten or fifteen years of rehearsal. Just write every day of your life. Read intensely. Then see what happens. Most of my friends who are put on that diet have very pleasant careers."

His second tip: stay away from journalism schools. "That's fatal. You don't learn a goddamn thing. Journalism has nothing to do with writing. The great newspaper writers are not journalists, they are essay writers.

"In fact, going to college to become a writer is the worst thing you can do, because you are not following your own tastes. What you need to do is develop your strong bent, whatever it is. If you are going to be a mystery writer, be a mystery writer. If you are going to write science fiction, write science fiction. But colleges don't understand that. They're not going to encourage you to do something that you love."

When he was starting out, even Bradbury had trouble doing what he wanted. Back in the forties he was writing for *Weird Tales*. "They wanted me to do a conventional ghost story. I told them I couldn't do that. I wanted to do the strangest things that popped into my head: the man who was afraid of the wind or the guy who was afraid of his skeleton.

"I had the same problem with the science fiction magazines. They were doing conventional, mechanical, technological pieces and many of them still are. I was writing human stories about little boys who want to grow up and become rocket men. What kind of science fiction story is that? It isn't at all."

Rather than being rejected, though, Bradbury's stories changed the nature of the market. His horror stories, written for fifteen, twenty-five, and thirty-five dollars for *Weird Tales*, are now gothic classics. The magazines that wouldn't publish Bradbury's new style of human science fiction died and the entire genre adjusted to make room for it.

In fact, the man who is billed on his book covers as "the world's greatest science fiction writer" is not really a science fiction writer at all. Editor Donald A. Wollheim said of his writing: "It has the form of science fiction, but in content there is no effort to implement the factual backgrounds. His Mars bears no relation to the astronomical planet. His stories are of people, real and honest and true in their understanding of human nature—but for his purposes the trappings of science fiction are sufficient—mere stage settings."

Critic Willis E. McNelly said of Bradbury: "His themes . . . place him squarely in the middle of the mainstream of American life and tradition. His eyes are set firmly on the horizon-Frontier where dream fathers mission and action mirrors illusion. And if Bradbury's eyes lift from the horizon to the stars, the act is merely an extension of the vision all Americans share."

His writing, particularly the stories based in Green Town, have a nostalgic air, a harkening to a time that we perceive as simpler. Yet, McNelly called it a "nostalgia for the future" and Bradbury, despite the homey, Midwestern, small-town settings of many of his stories, is definitely a city person with his eyes fixed on the next century. "We're going to rebuild all the cities of America during the next twenty years. We're on our way there now. All of this is due to the influence of people like Disney. He has taught the mayors of the world that their cities can be more human. They can have more gardens, more fountains, more places to sit. We are getting more interested in the quality of life. We're getting interested in rebuilding our cities and rebuilding our small towns. Parts of L.A. are being rebuilt right now. They're working on downtown San Diego. They're spending a *billion* dollars to humanize that."

Bradbury's affection for Walt Disney was reciprocated. When the Disney people were designing the Epcot Center at Disney World in Florida, they called on Bradbury for ideas. And at Disneyland's thirtieth anniversary celebrations, Bradbury was an honored guest.

His influence is long-term, touching several modern-day Disneys as well. For instance, in the 1960s, Bradbury spoke at a Southern California high school. Inspired by Bradbury's enthusiasm for movies, one young student turned to a friend and said, "I'm going to be the greatest filmmaker there ever was." Gary Kurtz went on to produce *American Graffiti, Star Wars, The Empire Strikes Back,* and *Dark Crystal.*

Bradbury speaks of many of today's creators as his "children" and some of them acknowledge it openly. "Are you still my papa?" Steven Spielberg asked Bradbury on their last meeting. "Yes," was the reply. "I'm still your papa."

"Do you have any idea of the number of lives you've changed?" I asked Bradbury.

"I have an idea it's quite a few."

It was then that I realized why I was crying. "I am one of your children, too," I said.

"I know," he told me. "I can see it in your face." And he stood up, came over to me and wrapped me in his arms. Not a wimp's arms at all but a father's arms, the arms of a man who has as many creative children as any author of his generation.

Thanks, Ray.

And thank *you*, Mr. Electrico.

section two

"NECESSARY LIES"
Why We Write What We Write

The best advice to writers is not the well-worn "Write what you know." It is "Write what you must."

The fact that the two pieces of advice are intimately intertwined is only, for the moment, a secondary concern.

Jack's Collar
by Lisa Garrigues

Lisa Garrigues wrote this piece about inspiration, about being a writer, "when I was a reluctant student in an English Comp class," she says—and I'll let her continue:

"I still feel very much in the process of becoming a writer, and hope that this feeling of 'becoming' will never leave me. I continue to get my 'attacks' of inspiration; I also continue to battle the demons of procrastination, doubt, distraction, and all those other things that keep me from the typewriter. My usual advice to myself—and to anyone else contemplating becoming a writer—is to just sit down and do it. And do it, and do it, and do it.

"The attacks continue, but perhaps I am less overwhelmed by them, knowing that the attack of inspiration is only the first, and easiest, stage in the business of writing. Once I've succumbed, I find myself digging deeper than I used to, finding the words beneath the words, the stories beneath the stories. This for me is part of the process of becoming a writer—a certain discontent with seeing the same thing twice, a desire to invent, and reinvent, the world as a place where literally anything can happen.

"So today the sun is out in San Francisco, and I'd love to be walking in Golden Gate Park, but there's a woman outside my window wearing a decidedly green dress, and before I know it I'm wondering what she's thinking, and . . . well, you know the rest."

This is the rest:

Somebody once asked me where I get my story ideas. I told him I don't get ideas. I get attacks.

I do my best to be like healthy people. I buy my food at the supermarket and my entertainment at the movies; I keep a steady job and my money in the bank. But no matter where I go, I live with the knowledge that anything in the environment might set me off.

Take Jack's collar, for instance.

Just last week I found myself, as even normal people do, in the midst of a cocktail party. All around me, people were engaged in conversation: A mauve dress wagged her finger up and down in the air in front of her face, chanting, "First you beat the eggs, then you cream the spinach, then you pound the meat, then you whip the sauce." A mustache followed the movement of her finger with rapt attention.

On the sofa, a fine head of curls leaned toward a leotard and drew concentric circles on his napkin with the end of his carrot stick. "It's like universal, you know . . . every circle encompasses another circle, every transformation encompasses another . . . everything is everything." The leotard nodded her head up and down like a toy in a Chinatown window. "That's intense," she murmured. "That's just too intense."

I was determined to be healthy and sociable at this party. I had just recovered from a massive attack the night before and did not need another one. A beige suit and tie asked me what I did in my spare time. I recited one of my favorite recipes. "It's universal," I added, and showed him the concentric rings I had sketched on my napkin with my forefinger and a dab of garlic dip. The beige suit was impressed. He said his name was Jack. I leaned toward him. "That's intense," I murmured, nodding my head rapidly.

I was doing fine. I could tell by the way Jack laughed that I was having a good time. He swirled his drink in his hand, jiggling the ice cubes. I swirled my drink; my ice cubes jiggled, too. I looked at the Chez Panisse poster on the wall and asked Jack if he didn't think it had "an interesting juxtaposition of blue and beige."

Jack turned his head. The skin of his neck folded over his collar. My mind caught on it like a snag. The skin. On his neck. Folded over his collar. Everything else stopped. I couldn't take my eyes off that little bulge of flesh that protruded nakedly from his white polyester shirt. My heart drummed in my chest like a basketball against concrete; my fingers began a curious, twitching dance. I knew I was about to have another attack. Before I could stop them, words began marching out of the crease that Jack's collar made against his neck. They crawled across the corner of his beige suit, buzzed around his gray mustache, and finally hovered directly in front of my face until I was forced to read them. There were huge gaps between them, and their syntax was sketchy, but as best as I could make them out, they looked something like this:

Jack stood next to the chip and dip table, wearing a shirt whose collar chafed his neck every time he turned his head. The cocktail party was a bore, but Jack was hoping he would meet someone there so he could go home and take off his shirt.

Lately, it seemed that all his shirts were just a little too tight, and all the parties he went to were just a little too crowded . . .

My jaw slackened, the color drained from my face, my eyes emptied. Jack was saying something about the "real motif" behind the Chez Panisse poster, but I could no longer hear him. The real Jack had been replaced by a fictional Jack who had already left the party with the woman in the mauve dress. By now, the words had swept into my mind and were churning around like leaves:

> Jack hated the word *mauve;* his ex-wife had used it. But she had used it so frequently, and with such a decisive pursing of the lips, that Jack knew *mauve* when he saw it. This woman's dress was definitely mauve. Jack could tell by the way she wore it that she too would call it mauve and not purple . . .

The real Jack was still moving his lips, but the thoughts of the fictional Jack were pounding so loudly between my ears that I had no idea what the real Jack was saying.

"Excuse me," I managed weakly, "I left someone at home."

Later, after I had spent an exhausting four hours at the typewriter with the fictional Jack and the woman in the mauve dress, I thought: Damn. If only he hadn't turned his head.

But there is always something, some murmur in the world around me that will set me off again. I am never safe. If I go to the supermarket and knock on a watermelon to see if it's ripe, my knock may be answered by a barrage of dialogue between two imaginary grocery checkers. If I go to the bank, an entire novel may leap at me from behind a teller's cage, or come creeping toward me from under a pile of papers on a loan officer's desk. If I go to a restaurant, hoping to satisfy my hunger with a fat, juicy hamburger, my entire meal may sit uneaten on my plate because of the phrase dangling from a single lock of hair on the waitress's forehead. No matter where I try to hide, I am always susceptible to another assault from another untold story.

So please, don't ask me where I get my ideas. I think I see one crawling toward me now, right off the end of your nose.

A postscript is in order here. Lisa writes, "Jack has since married and divorced the woman in the mauve dress and was last seen with a blonde blackjack dealer in Las Vegas. He's still having problems with his collar."

Hugging My Father, Myself
by David Strandin

To celebrate its sixtieth anniversary in 1980, Writer's Digest *invited its readers to enter a "What Writing Means to Me" contest, and then strait-jacketed them by limiting those thoughts to a mere five hundred words.*

"Mere" five hundred words, I say. A single word is like an ant—able to carry many times its weight. When a group of them of any size are chosen gracefully and well, their combined strength can be deceptively overwhelming. David Strandin understood that, and shed the strait jacket. He had no serious challenger in the contest.

In the Land of the Dead, living Odysseus attempted to embrace his dead father but hugged himself instead, his arms having passed through what he realized was only the spectre of his father's mortal form.

My bearded father, an underground iron mine carpenter with a frame so lean his miner friends nicknamed him "Bones" and with dancing brown eyes, like tiny promises in furrowed earth, ritually gathered my boyhood onto his lap after suppers and told me stories.

Sometimes he teased me with the story about the father who asked his son to tell him a story, and the son, in turn, told his father the story about the father who asked his son to tell him a story—and I laughed, because my father was my father and I was his son; we loved each other and we enjoyed the fiction about eternally recurring fathers and sons.

But boyhood and the after-suppertime storytelling ended when the iron mine carpenter was crushed by the weight of fallen friends, like so many trees charred and toppled by a subterranean conflagration that made the underworld a land of no return.

I inherited my father's love for stories.

I have found I am able to write the stories my father told, to recapture his voice, to relive my boyhood experience as audience—no matter that I now have a beard through which my own children crawl while I tell them stories. They explore their fantasies, believing that storytelling is endless.

And I write for my own children, and for myself, and for all fatherless children like me who have fathered children for whom childhood will one day end.

Writing is my way of crawling back onto my father's lap and discovering immortality, long after bones have turned to dust and ashes have blown away, leaving, not a scar, but a phoenix promise that will always be fulfilled as long as there are sages who tell stories, children who remember the sages in the words they write, and as long as there are gods in which to believe, even in a land of no return.

Odysseus hugged his father, himself, and became a wise man, the incarnation of his father's undying love.

Mortal Dreads
by Harlan Ellison

Harlan Ellison is every bit a literary wild man, in all positive senses of the phrase. He's the sort who would consider a stunt like sitting in a display window to write short stories in front of an audience, and then do it. And write good stories in the process.

Harlan Ellison is an editor: the landmark anthology Dangerous Visions *is his. He's a scriptwriter: for such shows as* Star Trek *and* Twilight Zone. *He's a fiction writer: "A Boy and His Dog," " 'Repent, Harlequin,' Said the Tick-Tock-Man," and "I Have No Mouth and I Must Scream" are considered classics.*

He's a fighter. He battles editors and television and other writers and his typewriter.

He battles himself, too.

And it makes for a very interesting bout.

With a touch of quiet pride, the Author states that he has watched the Johnny Carson show only once in his life. The single blot on an otherwise exemplary record occurred when I was pressed one night into sitting through consummate dreariness to reach the moment when Robert Blake, a friend of many years even though he's an actor, was to sit and talk to Orson Welles, one of my heroes despite his hawking of inferior commercial wines. It was a moment I wish had been denied me. Bob, a good and decent and talented man, clever, witty, and articulate, driven mad perhaps by the fame and cheap notoriety of having become a television cult hero for several seasons, proceeded to insult Mr. Welles in a manner I suppose he thought was bright badinage. It was a maleficent spectacle in overwhelming bad taste, culminating in Bob's passing a remark about Mr. Welles's girth.

Welles sat silently for a moment as the audience—and I—winced in disbelief and horror. Then he said, very softly, very softly, "My weight is correctable only with enormous difficulty at my age, but I live with it comfortably; as opposed to your bad manners."

There should be benign deities who would send ravens to pluck out one's eyes so such sights could be avoided.

I did not need to see my friend make an ass of himself. And I sat there thinking, for a wonder, is *this* what a vast segment of the American viewing public truly accepts as "the rebirth of conversation"? This endless babble and confluence of self-serving "celebrities" who warm studio sets with the indispensable intelligence that they'll be doing *Pal Joey* at the Country Squire Dinner Theatre in Lubbock, Texas, from June 12 to 18?

And I could not contain my sorrow that my friend had been driven mad by television, to sit there having been gulled into thinking he was having a "conversation" before so many millions of moon-white eyes in darkened bedrooms. But this time I will not inveigh against the Monster Video; that was the fulmination that served to introduce a collection of my stories in 1978, *Strange Wine*.

No, this time I would speak of conversation; of speaking to the true and universal darkness that fills so much of our soul. Of mortal dreads and the value of such terrors as I codify in fiction.

The extraordinary Peruvian novelist Mario Vargas Llosa— whose work, in particular *The Time of the Hero, Conversation in the Cathedral,* and *The Green House,* I urge you to discover—has said, "The writer is an exorcist of his own demons."

I proffer that unarguable observation, and these random thoughts about the commonly shared mortal dreads, in an effort to convey to any aspiring writers the warning that it is not enough merely to love literature, if one wishes to spend one's life as a writer. It is a dangerous undertaking on the most primitive level. For, it seems to me, the act of writing with serious intent involves enormous personal risk. It entails the ongoing courage for self-discovery. It means one will walk forever on the tightrope, with each new step presenting the possibility of learning a truth about oneself that is too terrible to bear.

While I believe it is true (as Malcolm Cowley has said), "No complete son of a bitch ever wrote a good sentence," I also concur, with William Faulkner, "If a writer has to rob his mother he will not hesitate; the *Ode on a Grecian Urn* is worth any number of old ladies." The tightrope sensibility stretching between these two apparently contradictory views is the thread of toughness a writer *must* be aware of, if s/he hopes to write with consequence. It is an awareness that demands an attitude of cynical optimism, uncompromising integrity, allegiance only to the work (not to film studios or publishers or readers or magazine editors) and, most of all, courage to explore the darkest places in oneself.

If we consider how readily and how easily all of us rationalize even the lightweight acts of cowardice in our daily lives, then by comparison we can see how terrifying it would be to come to grips with the innermost fears that scare the hell out of us. But it is precisely this complement of fears with which we must deal to write of the mortal dreads, the commonly shared emotional horrors that lie at the core of all human experience.

I'm not talking theory here. I'm talking about what Faulkner called the only thing worth the sweat and blood and anguish of writing: "the study of the human heart in conflict with itself." Because only in such study do we find the themes of fiction that are eternal, that command serious attention, that stand the test of time by which we judge great literature.

I do a considerable number of college lectures every year. They help pay the freight so I don't have to write television ever again. From my lips to the ear of God . . . or whoever's in charge.

And frequently I will say something about the human condition that seems perfectly rational and proper to me, because I know we all share the same thoughts. Invariably, some feep in the audience will attempt to pillory me with the stunning accusation, "You only said that to shock!"

My response is always the same:

"You bet your ass, slushface. Of course I said it to shock you (or *wrote* it to shock you). I don't know how *you* perceive my mission as a writer, but for me it is not a responsibility to reaffirm your concretized myths and provincial prejudices. It is not my job to lull you with a false sense of the rightness of the universe. This wonderful and terrible occupation of re-creating the world in a different way, each time fresh and strange, is an act of revolutionary guerrilla warfare. I stir up the soup. I inconvenience you. I make your nose run and your eyes water. I spend my life and miles of visceral material in a glorious and painful series of midnight raids against complacency. It is my lot to wake with anger every morning, to lie down at night even angrier. All in pursuit of one truth that lies at the core of every jot of fiction ever written: we are all in the same skin . . . but for the time it takes to read these stories I merely have mouth. You see before you a child who never grew up, who does not know it's socially unacceptable to ask, 'Who farted?' "

This I try to systematize in noble terms the obsession with Art and the inability of the writer to stop writing, to get along with others, to view without rancor the world as a gem, at once pure and perfect. But that's flapdoodle, of course. I write because I write. I can do no other.

It is the love of conversation.

I am anti-entropy. My work is foursquare for chaos. I spend my life personally, and my work professionally, keeping that soup boiling. *Gadfly* is what they call you when you are no longer dangerous, when the right magazines publish your work and you don't have to seek out obscure publications as homes for the really mean stuff, when they ask you to come and discuss matters of import with "celebrities" on the Johnny Carson show. I much prefer troublemaker, malcontent, pain in the ass, desperado. As I've said elsewhere, I see myself as a combination of Jiminy Cricket and Zorro. *Thus* do I ennoble myself in the times when all the simple joys I've forsworn rush back on me as chances lost, and I'm left with only the work and something Irwin Shaw said: "Since I am not particularly devout, my chances for salvation lie in a place sometime in the future on a library shelf."

Why is he telling me all this?

I'm telling you all this because if you are mad enough to want to spend your life behind a typewriter, locked in embrace with your dreams, you need to know that as they do with me, the feeps will think they're getting off a demolishing salvo when they accuse you of merely writing to shock.

I tell you all this to assure you none of us goes into the fray alone. It's our job: to stir the soup, to bite them on the thigh, to make them so angry it keeps the conversation going.

We live in a world that grows more constrained every day. From the moment you walk out onto the schoolyard at recess, the intent will be to make you fit in, to make you accept the status quo, to convince you that you are powerless. In other words, and not to be too extreme about it, the intent is to make you a coward.

You are sold a bill of goods that puts such intangibles as true love, security, being well liked, looking good and being "happy" (whatever the hell *that* means) at the top of the list of phantasms that must be pursued. Going for that kind of okeydoke will certainly guarantee that you will never write anything the feeps call shocking. You will become, at best, a creative typist, squandering your talent and your productive years writing the kinds of books and stories that can be sent to your mommy without worrying that she'll think she's raised a pervert.

I'm telling you all this because there are already enough rotten writers running loose without adding more cowardly hacks to the roster. By telling you this, by suggesting that greatness as a writer is seldom if ever achieved without danger, without taking the biggest

risks, I hope to scare off those of you who, like Willy Loman, treasure being "well liked" above the rewards one receives for having
written something that opens the sky.

The valuable writer is a night rider. A commando who slips in
when things are most quiet, and turns the night red with explosions.
Don't tell me what a nice story I wrote; I don't need that, I don't
want to hear it. Don't hum at me, don't invite me to parties for
pleasant chat. I want to hear the sound of your soul. Then I can
translate it into the mortal dreads we all share, and fire them back at
you transmogrified, reshaped as amusing or frightening fables.

Look, it's like this: I was in Utah doing some work for the
Equal Rights Amendment, and I said some things like this during a
radio interview. So the interviewer, who was a very bright guy,
pushed at it a little. He asked me to explicate some of these "mortal
dreads" that we all share, that I felt I was illuminating by writing
such weird and troubling stories. I thought about it a moment, and
then in a fit of confession that passes for honesty I told him about
writing the title story of my collection, *Shatterday.*

"I was sitting in a hotel room in New York in the middle of a
January snowstorm in 1975," I said. "I had to have the story finished by 7:00 that night so I could present it at a reading uptown at
7:30, allowing myself time to get a cab and find the auditorium . . .
and I was writing furiously, hardly thinking about how the story
was creating itself—"

The interviewer looked at me oddly.

"It was *creating itself?*"

"Yeah," I said. "I was just the machine that was putting it on paper. That story came out of secret places in my head and ran at the
paper without regard for my breaking back or the deadline. It
created itself. Well, I finished it barely in time, got downstairs,
shoved an old lady out of the way to grab her cab in the snow, and
just got uptown in time for the reading. I didn't even have time to
proofread the copy.

"So when I was in the middle of the lecture, reading the section
where the lead character is having the argument with his alter ego
about his mother, I realized for the first time that I wanted *my* mother to die."

The interviewer looked uncomfortable.

"No, wait, listen," I said hurriedly, "I didn't mean that I wanted
her to *die,* just to be gone. See, my mother was quite old at that time,
she'd been extremely ill off and on for years, and in that eerie way
we have of exchanging places with our parents when they grow old,

I'd become the parent and she'd become the child; and *I* was responsible for *her*. I supported her, and tried to keep her comfortable down in Miami Beach where she was living, and that gave me pleasure, to play at being grown-up son, and like that. But she was just a shadow. She hadn't been happy in a long time, she was just marking out her days, and I wanted to be free of that constant realization that *she was out there*. I loved her, she was a nice woman. I didn't have any rancor or meanness in me . . . I just had to admit that I wanted her gone."

The interviewer looked *really* uncomfortable now.

"Well, oh boy, that was some helluva thing to have to admit to myself. 'You slimy sonofabitch,' I thought, and I was still reading aloud to the audience that had no tiniest idea what monstrous and hellish thoughts were tearing me up. 'You evil, ungrateful, selfish prick! How the hell could you even *consider* something as awful as that? She never did anything to you, she raised you, put up with your craziness, and always had faith in you when everyone else said you'd wind up in some penal colony or the chipmunk factory! You sleazy, vomitous crud, how can you even *think* of her being dead?' And it was terrible, just terrible. I thought I was scum unfit to walk with decent human beings, to harbor these secret feelings about a perfectly innocent old woman. And I remembered what Eric Hoffer once wrote: 'What monstrosities would walk the streets were some people's faces as unfinished as their minds.'

"But there it was, in the story. I'd written it and had to confront it and learn to live with it." It was like the line out of another story in the new book, "All the Lies That Are My Life," where I mention the ugliness of simply being human. But I hadn't thought of that line then. And the interviewer didn't quite know what to say to me. What the hell can you say to some dude sitting there copping to wanting his mother to pass away?

Well, it was one of those call-in radio shows, and we started taking calls from Salt Lake citizens who were pissed off at an "outsider" coming in to tell them that Utah's not ratifying the ERA was a sinful and mischievous act. And then, suddenly, there was a woman on the line, coming over the headphones to me in that soundproof booth, with tears in her voice, saying to me: "Thank you. Thank you for telling that about your mother. My mother was dying of cancer and I had *the same thoughts* and I hated myself for it. I thought I was the only person in the world who ever thought such an awful thing, and I couldn't bear it. Thank you. Oh, thank you."

And I thought of that heart-rending scene in Jack Gelber's

play, *The Connection*, where the old Salvation Army sister, who has been turned into a medical junkie by inept doctors, says to this apartment full of stone righteous street hypes: "You are not alone. You are not alone."

I damned near started to cry myself. I wanted to hug that nameless woman out there in Salt Lake City somewhere, hug her and say *you are not alone*.

That's why I tell you all this.

You are not alone. We are all the same, all in this fragile skin, suffering the ugliness of simply being human, all prey to the same mortal dreads.

When I lecture I try to say this, to say most of the fears we invent—atomic war, multinational conspiracies, assassination paranoias, fear of ethnic types, flying saucers from Mars—those are all bullshit. I inveigh against illogical beliefs and say that the mortal dreads are the ones that drive you to crazy beliefs in Scientology, est, the power of dope, hatred of elitism and intellectual pursuits, astrology, messiahs like Sun Myung Moon or Jim Jones, fundamentalist religions. I try to tell you that fear is OK if you understand that what you fear is the same for *everyone*.

Not the bogus oogie-boogie scares of Dan O'Bannon and Ridley Scott's *Alien*, slavering creatures in the darkness that want to pierce your flesh with scorpion stinger tails and ripping jaws, but the fear of Gregor Samsa waking to discover he isn't who he was when he went to bed; the fear of Pip in the graveyard; the fear of Huck finding his dead father on the abandoned houseboat. The fears we are all heir to simply because we are tiny creatures in a universe that is neither benign nor malign . . . it is simply enormous and unaware of us save as part of the chain of life.

And all we have to stand between us and the irrational crazy chicken-running-around-squawking terror that those mortal dreads lay on us is wisdom and courage.

That is why I tell you all this, and why I write to shock and anger and frighten. To tell you with love and care that you are not alone.

My stories are about the mortal dreads.

Each one is a little different from all the others because, to fall back on words of Irwin Shaw again, " . . . in a novel or a play you must be a whole man. In a collection of stories you can be all the men or fragments of men, worthy and unworthy, who in different seasons abound in you. It is a luxury not to be scorned."

Yet the lure of that luxury is like a box of poisoned chocolates: sweet, but deadly.

For those who dabble at the craft, for those who have been making their way at cocktail parties for the last ten years delivering mouth-to-mouth resuscitation about the novel they're going to write, posing as "a writer" and occasionally turning out some piece of bad poetry to be read by friends and lovers who will praise it because they don't know any better, the lure of the dream of being a writer has nothing to do with the reality. Like whey-faced youths from the Kansas flatlands who arrive in Hollywood knowing nothing of the craft of acting, who desire only that nebulous catch phrase—*to be a star*—who can be found a year or two later decorating the singles' bars and psychobabble parties, the dilettantes who call themselves writers consign themselves to lives of endless hunger.

Writing is the hardest work in the world.

I have been a bricklayer and a truck driver and I tell you—as if you haven't been told a million times already—that writing is harder. Lonelier. Nobler and more enriching.

But what you need to know, that they may never have told you, is that it is dangerous. It demands courage and heart. Not just to keep writing and sending out the work in hopes someone who can put it in print will give you the nod, but the courage to give years of your life to exploring the mortal dreads that make a piece of fiction an illuminating experience.

And there is only one note of reassurance that counts. . . .

Honest to God—or whoever's in charge—you are not alone.

California Sweet, or My Hitherto Undivulged Secret Magnetic Process of Constructing Magazine Articles
by Maurice Zolotow

*I could spend a while explaining to you what Maurice Zo-
lotow has accomplished as a writer, but this article explains that far better than I could. I could spend even more
time describing Zolotow's technique for building articles
from foundation to pinpoint pinnacle, but, again, the best
explanation lies in the writing itself. . . .*

For a long time I struggled with the construction of magazine
articles, even though I wrote and sold hundreds of them. It is only
within the last few years, since I moved to Los Angeles and became a
Hollywood magazine and book writer, that illumination has struck.
I learned my secret magnetic process of fashioning pieces, which not
only speeded up the process but also enhanced the form, quality,
and utter charm of my articles. I would, like you, and you and most
of all, *you*, agonize, sometimes for hours and days, hurling crude,
clumsy, unworkable leads into the air. God, there must be thousands of crumpled page ones in my past. And then, after I left New
York, after my wife divorced me for very good grounds (I was quite
impossible to endure), and I emigrated to the West Coast, I gradually ceased agonizing over leads. Nowadays, I write (in my mind) the
ending of the article *before* I write the lead—and suddenly there is
no more agony over leads. No more squashed page ones. Nowadays, I compose an entire article in my mind before I repose in the
chair and gently tap the keys of the typewriter. And it all flows.
　　You know those horseshoe-shaped magnets, don't you? Well,
the lead is like one curve of the magnetic horseshoe and the conclu-

sion is the other, like New York and Los Angeles are also the prongs of my emotional magnet, and when you work with this invisible magnet, all the little metal filings—all the pieces of data, fragments of dialogue, all the little shreds—are drawn to the poles and form a design, almost by themselves. Now I wonder why, in my writing and when I would take a workshop in a summer writers conference or lecture at one of those day-long conferences, I would become obsessed with the lead and somehow forget the ending, the last paragraph, the final sentence, the summing up, the resolution of it all, the ultimate satisfaction of the reader when he experiences the filings as a pretty design. All of us live in negative and positive, or Yin and Yang, for it is in the nature of being—and two cities are always in us, the place where we were born and reared and the place where we have settled, and New York used to be my positive and LA my negative, but now it is reversed and has been for ten years.

Most of the time I forget the passage of the years and get to take for granted this way of life I have now, in Hollywood. Sometimes, though, something gives me a shock, and I see my present life from a momentarily detached viewpoint, my New York frame of mind takes over, and I know that the man with my name who came from NY ten years ago would regard me as I am now as an authentic Southern California flake. I still have NY in me somewhere. A recent shock was getting my renewal from the triple A, known hereabouts as the Automobile Club of Southern California. The AAA sent me not only the card but also a sticker to put on the windshield: *Member Over Ten Years.* That's when it hit me. A decade! I live in the same four-room flat overlooking Fountain Avenue, a block below that section of Sunset Boulevard we call the "Sunset Strip."

I can look out of the picture window of my terrace and see an enormous magnolia tree that bears white blooms all summer long. The leaves are glossy and green all through the year. I'm so used to the absence of autumn and winter that I really forget how it is back in NY or Chicago or Boston. That magnolia tree is in the courtyard of a strange French provincial clump of little white castle-shaped apartment houses, the place being called the Chateau Frontenac. How I used to sneer at this Hollywood type of pseudo-Gothic and pseudo-Tudor and pseudo-French Provincial. Now I adore ever turret and conical tower and gabled window of the Chateau Frontenac and I love all those other crazy buildings put up during the baroque Hollywood period of the 1920s. It's part of the landscape of my body and it has gotten into my mind. I take for granted the fat shaggy palm tree I can see out of the dining room window facing west.

It's on Hacienda Street. The streets of my milieu are named Olive, Flores, Sweetzer, Selma, Crescent Heights, Fairfax . . . fantasy trees like palms and bananas and fantasy buildings and fantasy street names and I love them. And all the trees bearing lemons and avocados, right in the heart of West Hollywood, which I pass on my morning's walk from which I've just returned. It is the middle of April and it must be getting close to 90° F.

And the events of my life really would seem quite weird to the former person who bore my name. I get up between 6 and 6:30 A.M. I haven't had a Seconal the night before. I haven't had a sleeping pill in nine years. I used to start my days at about 11 A.M. and usually had a scotch and soda. I haven't had a drink of alcohol, not even wine or beer, in nine years. The MZ of eleven years ago would have had no truck with this MZ of today.

My breakfasts are large and I usually have a fresh orange or grapefruit and bran toast and a couple of eggs and ham and coffee and many vitamin pills. Then I walk for a mile or two. I never used to walk. I never had a healthy breakfast and I was not too crazy about healthy dinners or lunches either.

Now if you want to know how flaky I am, I'll reveal to you that about once a week I go to see Zion Yu. Zion Yu is a marvelous Chinese acupuncturist and he gives me the needles—about sixty to seventy of them—all over my head and face and neck and torso and genital area and my thighs, legs, and ankles. I have been a patient of Dr. Yu's for seven years. First I went for muscular aches and pains and stiff joints but I feel good now and I just go to him for "balancing my Yin/Yang."

Can you picture me—cynical, skeptical Manhattan man—loving acupuncture treatments, really believing in Yin and Yang, positive and negative, leads and conclusions?

Parking is rarely a problem in LA. I park on the street wherever I go, to Dr. Yu's or wherever.

Sometimes after a treatment, I have to go out and do some research, but doing it here is so different. So relaxed. So—ah!—laid back. Yeah, like I'm getting to be real laid back. But "laid back" doesn't mean loafing. *Au contraire,* I write harder and more productively and enjoy it more. Some highlights of the last few weeks were definitely on what the old MZ would have called the weird side. Like one morning I drove over the hills into the San Fernando Valley to an abandoned schoolhouse on Buena Vista Avenue. This was being used as a location for several sequences in the George Burns movie in which he again plays God. The title of the picture is

Oh God, Book II. John Denver isn't in this one. The human to whom God reveals Himself is a little girl of ten who is played by a little girl of ten named Louanne and who doesn't use her surname professionally. And the sun was bright and the sky blue and decorated with lovely clouds and it was warm even though it was March. I have already forgotten how it was back on East 44th Street, Manhattan, where I lived at the Beaux Arts Hotel, after the separation, and used to meet stars and other subjects on freezing mornings or afternoons, usually in restaurants or office buildings. And now I'm sitting around in the sun in the playground of this public school watching director Gilbert Cates put the cast through their paces. I am writing a profile of George Burns for *Reader's Digest.* I talked to little Louanne. I waved to Suzanne Pleshette and conversed with David Birney, who play her parents in the picture. And it was all so casual and laid back and amiable.

Everybody says *Have a nice day* around here.

And we do.

I hardly remember how nervous, wretched, frantic, miserable human beings are in NY. But still there's that NY guy hiding inside me, as well. Negative pole.

Usually I do the interviews in the afternoon and the writing in the morning. Sometimes I go to a library in Beverly Hills or the Motion Picture Academy of Arts Library on Wilshire. I always find a place to park and nothing is crowded. There are no crowds out here. I was sitting at my desk the other morning when Rubin Carson phoned. Carson is another Hollywood correspondent. We went to a luncheon given to honor the memory of Rasputin by the International Rasputin Society at the Kavkaz on Sunset Boulevard. Doesn't that confirm every prejudice about Hollywood the land of crazies? Yeah—and I guess I'm one. Because I had a ball at this homage to Rasputin. Paul Valentine, a huge actor, was wearing a Rasputin disguise and there were speeches and we had *zakuski,* Russian *hors d'oeuvres,* or *horse's ovaries* as an old girlfriend used to call them, and there was a gang of media people and photographers and Rubin and I took our plates of *zakuski* and found a table out in the patio in back and sat beneath the fronds of a pepper tree and we engaged in repartee with two women producers who did shows for the Osmond family—you know, Donny and Marie and their siblings and relatives. And all the time, my brain is typing words. I don't have an assignment on Rasputin but wherever I go and whatever I do, I carry in my head an Olivetti electric portable that is clicking away, for whatever my senses experience it seems that I must instantly transform into syllables, most of which I'll never get to put on paper and sell, but I don't care, and it wouldn't matter if I did, because I've come to see it's my nature. That's part of the education I've gotten since I moved to California.

A few days later I went to a 6 P.M. party for George Burns and Louanne, a joint birthday party, celebrating his eighty-fourth year and her eleventh year at Liu's on Rodeo Drive. It used to be Mike Romanoff's, one of the glamorous restaurants and watering holes of Hollywood's golden age.

There was a bigger horde of photographers at Liu's than there was at the party for Rasputin. The food here was a big plate of *dim sum*, which are Chinese *zakuski* or *horse's ovaries*, if you will. By the way, I drank Perrier water with a slice of lime wherever I went. Yes, I'm one of these Perrier imbibers now. They cut a cake. Louanne cut it and gave a slice to George Burns. Burns took it over to his booth. He munched on barbecued spareribs and other delicacies on his plate. He had some cake. He finished his second martini. Then he lit a cigar. He smiled and ogled beautiful women in Hollywood. I guarantee it. I always feel very old when I'm around George Burns. He asked me if I had read his new book. I said I had and loved it. I think I will write a nice article about Burns for *Reader's Digest*. In fact, I'm writing parts of it right now in my head and I know how I'm going to end it and I think I've got my lead, yes, yes, I have it, my lead.

And a few weeks later, I was preparing an article on Arthur Betz Laffer, an economics professor at the University of Southern California. I was writing this for the July issue of *Los Angeles* magazine. Dr. Laffer is the discoverer of the Laffer Curve, which allegedly proves that lower taxes produce higher government revenue. He is the brains behind Ronald Reagan's economic planning. He is the man who devised the 30 percent tax cut incentive plan. How did I get in touch with Professor Laffer, one of the most important econometricians in the U.S., an advisor to many large corporations and pension funds and mutual funds? I just called his office at U.S.C. and was put right through to him. He didn't know me from Adam—Adam Smith that is. But he was right friendly, which we are in Southern California, and I set up an appointment to interview him at his home in Rolling Hills, and subsequently to sit in on one of his graduate seminars in macro-economics. So there I was, rolling along the Santa Ana Freeway to Rolling Hills and soon I was talking to Professor Laffer on the rear patio of his simple and typical California ranch house. We were calling each other "Art" and

"Maurice" right away. Dr. Laffer, it turned out, is a bird lover and collects tropical birds and our conversation was interrupted by frightening screams from various macaws and toucans flying about or caged on the premises. He is a member of the Audubon Society and the Tortuga Club, the latter being a group of persons who love turtles. Laffer had many turtles trudging in his beautiful garden of cactuses and succulents. Yes, my friends and fellow writers, that is how one interviews subjects in Los Angeles. Do you really think I would ever wish to work in any other ambiance?

Not long after my encounter with toucans and turtles and Laffer, I had occasion to visit with Neil Simon, who is an old acquaintance. Simon, playwright and screenwriter, is the author of *The Odd Couple, The Sunshine Boys, California Suite,* and other works too humorous to mention. In New York, I would probably have queried Simon in the hectic atmosphere, the noise and clutter of Sardi's. I wanted to ask Neil his recollections of Walter Matthau for *Reader's Digest.* And where did we meet? Why, on the patio of the Beverly Hills Tennis Club. Where else? Simon is a passionate tennis player. He has his office near the club so he can get in a few sets after a morning of composition. There are no turtles at the tennis club. There were tennis players on the courts and swimmers in the pool. And we sat out there, he in shorts and I in slacks, and of course we weren't wearing ties or coats (nor had Laffer been wearing any either), and we talked about what an acting genius and lovely comic spirit Matthau was, while we sipped iced tea and basked in the sun. Naturally I saw Matthau himself many times and in many places and one of the places was the Hollywood Park Race Track where we spent a whole day and I won $24, which is not much, but is better than a sharp stick in the eye. (Oh, I just noticed that it is 9:30 A.M. and it is time for my lotus break. I've got a lotus plant growing on my balcony and if you'll just hold the phone I'll go get a leaf and munch it while I tell you more about my curious Hollywood life.)

Well, I'm back now. It sure tastes sweet—the lotus, I mean. Oh yes, Matthau, *A Day at the Races* starring Walter Matthau. Well, would you believe it? A few weeks later, I was testing a new horserace computer device for *Los Angeles* magazine. The piece was to run in September. I took it out to Hollywood Park with another friend, not an actor, an architect. The computer picked four winners in the seven races it handicapped. A week later it did even better— yielding me a $75 profit. So I decided last week I had to get away for a few days from all this hard work I have to do, so I took my little computer (whom I have nicknamed Supertout) to Del Mar, a little track down by the sea, whose slogan is, "Where the surf meets the turf." I was there for four days. On August 21, a Thursday it was, I had the single greatest and most fulfilling day of my sporting life. I hit a $91 daily double (the horses were named Nino and Head Lad, if you're interested) and in the seventh race I had Western Hand and Kirby Muxloe in the Exacta and they came in and it was a $428.50 Exacta. . . .

I have decided not to mention that fascinating lunch I enjoyed with Bob Hope at his gorgeous estate in Toluca Lake because you'll start drooling and I can just see hundreds and hundreds and maybe thousands of freelance writers trekking to Los Angeles from all over the place. Well, ladies and gentlemen, take it easy. It's not all iced tea with Neil Simon and coffee and turtles with Art Laffer and $428.50 Exactas. Listen—we got *earthquakes* out here, yeah, and terrible typhoon rains and mudslides and these godawful brush fires in summer and that smog is a killer. So if you're thinking of moving out here—*Don't*. The prices on homes are going through the roof—which naturally causes leaks and you can't find apartments at any price. *Stay home.*

(Whew, I'm glad I thought of bringing this up; otherwise there would be hordes of literary aspirants messing up this earthly paradise.)

So I was telling you about this article on horse-race computers that I wrote for *Los Angeles*. I've gotten to love Las Vegas since I moved to LA. I go there four, five times a year to play blackjack, poker, and other games of chance and to write about the Las Vegas action. I think I'm going to write an article about poker-playing champions of Vegas in *Playboy*. The last article I had in *Playboy* was about blackjack in Vegas. I can't picture myself going to Vegas without having an idea to write about. In fact, it is impossible for me to go anywhere without writing in my head. I've never really had a vacation, since I cannot suspend the activity of my brain and really don't want to. I love writing. I love thinking about it and I love doing it as I am doing it at this moment. After I left Burns, I thought about Louanne and about child actors, there being so many of them now. Later that month I'd have an interview with Jackie Coogan, who was one of the greatest and most famous child movie stars of all time, and was internationally famous during the 1920s. I was working on a portrait of Jackie Coogan, who is still a sharp guy, for *50 Plus Magazine*, for which I occasionally do profiles of persons like Buddy Ebsen, Mary Martin, Art Carney. George Burns is still too young for *50 Plus*.

Now guess who I met in the elevator when I came home to my apartment? Lita Gray Chaplin and her husband Art. She was Chaplin's second wife and the mother of two of his sons. She is a charming lady who is a sportswear buyer at Robinson's department store. She must be seventy-five years old. She has almost as much energy and verve as George Burns. I told her I'd been speaking with Jackie Coogan (who had acted opposite her former husband in the classic movie, *The Kid*). Lita told me she had played a small part in *The Kid* and later sang with a jazz band Jackie organized in the 1930s.

"Jackie was six and I was twelve," she said wistfully about the making of *The Kid*.

About the same age Louanne is now, I thought.

Lita Gray Chaplin's yellow VW (license plate LITA G C) is parked three vehicles away from my white 1970 Maverick (007-BBF) in our underground garage.

When I start viewing my life in New York terms I can see how bizarre it looks. The other night for instance, I went over to Sheldon Keller's house, high up in the Hollywood Hills over on Astral Drive. Keller is coauthor of the George C. Scott picture, *Movie Movie*. He is an amateur Dixieland musician. He plays tuba in a band known as the Beverly Hills Unlisted Jazz Band. They practice at his house one or two nights a week. Movie star George Segal sings vocals and plays banjo and Conrad Janis plays tailgate trombone. Janis played Mindy's father in "Mork and Mindy." I think I'll write a little *causerie* about Segal, Janis, Keller, and this crazy little band for *People* magazine.

I imagine you are beginning to think that maybe *everything* I do, everything I hear, see, smell, touch, taste, has to be written up in an article.

Damn right.

That's one of the discoveries I have made about myself since I became a California flake.

I used to think I wrote in order to live. I was wrong. I live in order to write and everything I experience has to become words. The best hours of my life are when I am forming the words into sentences and shaping the paragraphs and letting the magnetic poles, the leads and the conclusions, draw the filings into a pattern. I never get homesick for New York. Last night I went over to the Twentieth Century-Fox studio on Pico Boulevard to see a press screening of a new film. I passed the *Hello Dolly* set with the false fronts of old Manhattan and the vanished Third Avenue Elevated R.R.

This is as close as I get to NY these days.

This is as close as I want to get to it.

I never believed this could happen—that I could exist happily in any other place than New York City.

I was born again here in LA.

Louanne and I, in a way, share an eleventh birthday.

And, my friends, this is the conclusion I had in my mind before I devised the lead for the article you have been reading and this is what it was all meant to mean, the finale of it.

So do you get the east and the west of it, the negative and the positive, the Yin of it?

Do you get the Yang and the Hang of it, now, do you?

Funny Stuff
by Julie Wheelock

Julie Wheelock is something of an improv artist. You've seen those comedians who will improvise a funny scene on the spot, basing it on little more than a couple of props, or perhaps just a subject. Jonathan Winters is a master at that sort of comedy. So is the Second City comedy troupe.

Give Julie a topic, and she'll turn around and supply a comic essay—on deadline, and funny. Few writers can do that. But then, that's Julie's calling, as she herself now explains.

Last week a friend and I went to a publication party, one of those quasi-literary affairs where people walk around clutching plastic glasses of lukewarm white wine and eye each other, wondering who might be important and worth cultivating as a contact. You can always tell the truly important ones because they check their watches a lot and duck out early.

The author, with plastic smile and glassy eyes, was autographing books at a Lucite table, surrounded by politely jostling guests claiming prior acquaintance.

"Oh, you must remember, it was at your reading last year. I was the one who admired your analogies."

Since we're not yet literary hotshots, we were surprised when a man from the group walked over to talk to us.

"So, what kind of writing do you do?" he asked, knocking back his wine with a déclassé gulp.

That's a question writers often hear, and by now I've learned to be succinct. No one seems to understand me when I say, "Funny stuff." I guess they think that's a nonanswer. They need something specific, like sports or seventeenth-century drama. So I said what I usually say, "Um, humor."

He looked unimpressed and turned to my friend. "How about you?"

"I'm writing a novel," she said.

"Oh, really? A novel! Well! How long is it? Say, I've got this terrific story idea I'd like to talk over with you. . . ."

Well, you can guess what happened to the three-way conversation after that. A third of it suddenly became inaudible. There's something about the word *novel* that summons forth great quantities of respect, awe, and admiration. A novel is major-league, the big time. It's proof that you're serious about writing. And the best part is that you don't actually have to finish one in order to get attention; it's enough just to *say* you're writing one. If anyone tries to check up on you, you can carry around a little cardboard box of paper that you call your manuscript, and you say something like, "It's not quite in final draft yet, but when it is I'll let you have first look."

I'm not sure just what's going on, but lately I've seen a lot of people carrying notebooks and pens, and sometimes little cardboard boxes. They sit around in parks, restaurants, and malls, mostly staring into space. Unless it's a new kind of social behavior, I guess they're all writing, trying to write, or putting on literary airs.

If you ask them what they're writing, they usually look up, pause for dramatic effect and say, "I'm working on My Novel."

By the way they say it, you know the words are capitalized. They never say, "I'm working on my How-to Book," or "I'm writing my Human Potential Book." It's always, "I'm working on My Novel."

When my friend says it, I don't know how she knows. I mean, she's never written one before, so how can she tell whether it's a novel, a novella, a short story, or a cereal box?

Whatever her project, however, I think she's got a great all-purpose rationale for dealing with life. For example, she can say, "I'm working on My Novel, so I can't 1) answer the phone, 2) clean the house, 3) walk the dog, 4) pay the bills, 5) jog, or 6) listen to anyone.

She gets to be antisocial ("I haven't time."), hypersocial ("I'm only at this party to gather material."), apathetic ("I'm stuck."), even hysterical ("I'm *blocked!*").

Her response to every human condition or predicament is, "But I'm working on My Novel."

I have to admit that I envy her. I'd like to be able to work on My Novel and say all those things, too. But that isn't what I write. I'm not a novelist. I write short funny stuff, a thousand words, max. That's just the kind of writer I am.

I've tried. One day I sat down in the park with a notebook and pen and stared into space. In sixty seconds of free association I had the following thoughts:

Irving Wallace, Judith Krantz, and Harold Robbins go for the big money. So can I. It's easy if you forget about writing as a fine art and stick to The Formula: violence, money, and sex. Well, maybe a little funny stuff, to take the edge off.

But violence makes me queasy. Forget the violence. Money and sex? What do I know about money? Forget the money. OK, there's sex. Maybe sex and a trendy location. Sex on Rodeo Drive? No, more international. Sex and Cap d'Antibes? Passé. Maybe sex and Saskatoon? What about sex and funny stuff? Sex and the garage sale: Sex at the library? Sex and the Little League? Forget the sex.

Well, that about wraps up my try at the big time. Item by item I ruled out The Formula and ended up with what I usually write. I think those writing experts who advise us to stick to what we do best are right.

However, I still want attention. I'm beginning to think it's probably just a matter of attitude, and I'm pretty sure I can pull it off. The next time someone asks me what I write, I'm going to look up, pause, and say, "I'm working on my Funny Stuff."

I may not get respect, awe, and admiration, but I'll settle for laughs.

Necessary Lies
by Martha Grimes

Martha Grimes has in recent years been touted as one of the best women writers of mysteries, her name appearing in lists alongside P. D. James, Dorothy Salisbury, and Ruth Rendell. I'll readily agree with that, though mystery buyers don't seem to care terribly whether a writer is male or female, so why should the critics?

That's a small side point; the main point to consider here is why her novels are so popular. I think it's because she has a compassion to her writing, a compassion marvelously evident in this story of research and the need to ignore it for the good of the book.

When I saw him standing on a dark and windy corner in Whitehall asking directions to New Scotland Yard, I knew he was for me. With an awful air of desperation, he was stopping passers-by, who shook their heads and walked on.

"All I know is that it's on Victoria Street," I told him. "I've been looking for it too for the last hour."

"Well, *come* on, then, luv," he said, as if I'd been late and holding him up for hours. "I've got the old banger parked over there. We'll just drive round till we find it. I've got to get to Scotland Yard. Someone's trying to poison me."

Why was I surprised? Detective Chief Inspector Richard Jury, whose fictional career I've been tracking in my novels, would have thought it all in a night's work, although Jury doesn't usually encounter potential victims/murderers/suspects on windy street corners; when Jury finds them, they're either dead and not talking, or sitting in front of a crackling fireplace over tea and biscuits, talking six-to-the-dozen about all the other potential victims/murderers/suspects in whatever cozy village I send him to.

Not that my street-corner friend, a junk dealer from the coast, wasn't a talker. As we drove up and down Victoria Street, stopping to roll down the windows and ask directions to the Yard, he told me in florid detail his baroque tale of arsenic-in-the-casserole.

Serves me right, I thought, for writing traditional arsenic-in-the-tea British detective novels.

It occurred to me that this wasn't the healthiest way of doing research—jumping into old bangers in the dark with strangers, especially ones who claim they're being slowly poisoned. But I'd been having a lot of trouble collecting information about Scotland Yard. I found the books written about it helpful only up to a point. Former superintendents and ex-commissioners want to write about their most famous cases, not about the often dull round of the policeman's day. I have even gone through several Reports of the Commissioner—soporific in their regard for minutiae, but, then, the commissioner doesn't plot out his reports to the Queen with a cast of squirrelly characters and a Christie-like denouement.

My next attempt to gather technical information was through a chatty letter to the Public Information Office. Nothing doing. You don't chat up Scotland Yard. Awfully naive of me, but I assumed it was like the FBI, with all sorts of touristy things laid on. I was informed (rather huffily) that Scotland Yard is not a public building, not a separate entity, but the headquarters for the Metropolitan Police. There were no facilities for writers and no tours. He clearly thought it pretty cheeky of an American to encroach upon British territory, both literally and metaphorically. If I didn't know anything about another country's police force, why was I trying to write about it?

I tried a less formal approach. When I was lucky enough to meet a reformed thief (the extent of the reformation being questionable), I decided to go in, as it were, by the back door. Unfortunately, all of his contacts decided to go out this way. Every "appointment" he had set up for me found me all by myself, either sitting in the pub waiting, or in the doorway waiting, or on a Thames-side dock waiting. It was lonely being thought of, apparently, as an undercover agent wearing the *persona* of a mystery writer.

Now, I was certainly not under the impression that my new friend, the junk dealer, would open doors magically for me. I had to inform him, as we careened into the driveway in front of the plate-glass-and-steel building on a lopped-off corner of Victoria Street, that the police constable on duty was probably not the doorman. The PC, in somewhat more trenchant tones, told him the same thing in language Inspector Jury and his fictional colleagues would never dream of using. But, of course, Jury's Watson, Melrose Plant (ex-earl, ex-viscount) could have brought off our operation with far more élan. In one of my books, he does indeed drive up in his Rolls, hands the policeman on duty a few quid, and says, "Park it anywhere, old chap."

Funny, we didn't think of that; we just parked on the street like "real" people. We returned to the entrance, went inside and ran up against a phalanx of desks and constables and clerks. I cringed as they asked my friend his business, largely because they thought I must be part of it. The constable showed how much training must go into keeping one's face expressionless as my companion related his odyssey, ending up (rather tactlessly, I thought) with an account of how corrupt the provincial police force was in his county. They were in on casserole-poisoning, too.

I stared at the air and pretended I hadn't come in with him, that we had just met by accident in the revolving door. The constable asked him to go into the waiting room; I drifted over to the information desk.

In a few minutes, a couple of brisk-looking detectives got off one of the lifts and swanned over to my friend. I was close on their heels, but they managed to surround him.

So I sat down to wait and wonder what my relentless sleuthing after "truth" was all about. Does the reader really want to know there is *no* Murder Squad? No clever little clique of inspectors, kept separate and above the grime of London's streets, who go whisking off to places like my fictional village to foil some equally clever criminal? Does the reader want to know the extent of police corruption in London? Does he want to know that the Yard really isn't called in to solve especially sticky cases out in the provinces—not even in the case of the Yorkshire Ripper?

What a beating the neo-"Golden-Age" detective novel would take. We'd have to call back Appleby and Alleyn, Dover and Dalgleish, and force them to toil in London. They could no longer slog through the insular and claustrophobic English village, crossing the village green, chatting with the village vicar, invading the village Manor, feeling the veil of village rain, and having a best bitter in the village pub. For the fans of this particular subgenre of the mystery novel, all of that is the stuff of dreams.

And those two real detectives over there, now rising from their seats, would never recognize Inspector Richard Jury as a co-worker. He moves too slowly, is too affable and urbane, spends too much time listening to suspects, uses his powers of deduction without much visible aid from ballistics and forensics. Those two over there, with the sophisticated equipment and methods of the police, and the suspects lined up neatly like ducks in a row, could solve the crime before the tea was half-drunk. But where's the fun in that?

Thus Jury is not really "real," except for me and (I hope) the reader, whose willing suspension of disbelief works with this sort of mystery if it ever works at all. And, yet, it is more than that: it is not simply that the reader accepts the conventions, but that he *demands* them. The traditional English mystery is not a police procedural. Although I wanted to *know* the red-tape details, I didn't want to *use* them. My sort of mystery is far more an exercise in deduction and an occasion to give free play to a dozen or so cranky types than it is a "true" account of how Scotland Yard operates.

The detectives departed; my friend walked back across the lobby. "They said if I wanted the hair and fingernail test, I could go to any hospital," he told me. "Well, that's bloody untrue, innit? I did try to go to one, but they wouldn't take me, would they? I know why. The local police told them I was coming." Sadly, he added, "They didn't believe me."

Jury would have.

section three

"COUNSEL FROM A VETERAN OF THE WRITING WARS"

Some Words of Advice

If you could pose one question to a successful writer, what would it be?

Whatever it is, it's probably answered in the articles of counsel included in the next few pages.

Counsel from a Veteran of the Writing Wars
by Irving Wallace

Irving Wallace is a writer whose name on the cover of a book almost assures the book's placement on the bestseller list. But more than just those two words must appear; thousands of words, carefully placed, must go into each volume.

But is careful placement of words enough? Irving Wallace says no, and then explains the other ingredients essential to the success not only of a book, but also of the book's author.

I once overheard a professor say to a beginning writer: "Everything has been written about already, and written better than you can do it. If you intend to write about love, tragedy, adventure . . . forget it, because it has all been done by Shakespeare, Dickens, Tolstoy, Flaubert, and the rest. Unless you have something absolutely new to say, don't try to be a writer. Take up accounting."

That was silly—really stupid. Everything has not been said, and will never be said. Human emotions may have always been the same. Still, there was never anyone on earth before you who was exactly like you and who saw love and hate exactly as you see them through your eyes.

And you need not have lived something to see it, to write about it. You were provided with imagination. Use it. Da Vinci did not have to attend the Last Supper to paint it.

Use your imagination daily. Writing is not only an art but also a profession. While inspiration is an enormous factor, the writing of a book is a profession. You have to prepare for this profession by practicing it—write diaries, journals, letters, fragments—and by studying the works of authors you admire, to learn how they create characters, insert conflict, move a story.

And then you have to write not just when the spirit moves you, but every day. If there are bad days, you can discard what you've done, but write every day, pretending you're on a salary, pretending you must deliver something or be fired, yet working on and on for yourself and by yourself.

When I was doing short magazine pieces and screenplays, I feared undertaking anything as formidable as a book. One day, while I was collaborating with novelist Jerome Weidman on a screenplay for a studio, Weidman advised me how to overcome my fear. "Think about writing one page, merely one page, every day. At the end of 365 days, the end of a year, you have 365 pages. And you know what you have? You have a full-length book."

Finally, you must want to write rather than to be known as a writer. That's why you must treat your actual writing as a career. You must not talk about it. You must do it—want to do it, love to do it despite the loneliness, feel there is nothing more important on earth while you are doing it.

Because there is nothing more important. Despite what that professor contended, there are things left to be said. The world around you is different from the world Shakespeare wrote about—your world today has trod on the moon, by God. For every new writer, every new year remains unexplored until he or she explores it.

A Journey of a Thousand Miles Begins with a Single Slip

by Jeff Taylor

The surest way of getting a rejection slip from Writer's Digest *is to send us a story about rejection slips. We get dozens of such stories, and they're usually woe-is-me tales that their authors hope we will see as woe-are-us tales that all writers will relate to.*

Jeff Taylor's piece was the buyable exception. He took the subject of rejection slips, held it in front of a mirror to get a different perspective, shook it hard so that all the related clichés fell from it like rust flakes, and wondered how he might replace the clichés with fresh insights and useful instruction.

That was, according to the thesis forwarded here, a mistake, and he knew it when he received our acceptance letter. "Darn," he wrote back to me. "Oh, well. Thanks for the gentle letdown—this sale discouraged me less than most."

So, as we said in the subhead to this article when we originally printed it, go out and lose one for the Gipper.

When I first attempted writing for publication, I was given The Secret of Success: "You'll never succeed as a writer until you have a thousand rejection slips."

This edict came from my father, a sale-shocked veteran of too many deadline staredowns with his typewriter. Once, over several drinks, a great writer revealed to him the magic formula of the Inner Circle. He passed it along to me, with the warning that it might seem an impossible goal.

My father quit writing in 1960, and went into life insurance, which was more of a sure thing, he said. "After all," he told me, "you can't guarantee that an editor won't buy some dumb idea of yours, if it's well written and he needs it. But I can absolutely promise my clients that it's just a question of time before they die, and there's a lot of satisfaction in that. And believe me, the Grim Reaper pays well and reliably, compared to the Muses."

Poor old Pop. He'd made a living by writing, but was never a success. Oh, he'd been a gypsy writer and feature editor, and had broken into the national magazine market in the fifties. But the thousand-nope figure was, for him, unattainable. He hit a hundred early on, before a streak of sales demoralized him. Over the years, he has managed to collect only a third of the Secret Number.

He still writes a few pieces every season or so. They usually sell. It must tear him up inside to know that, at his age, he'll never see his thousandth rejection slip. But my father's a tough old pretzel. Somehow, he manages to smile when the checks come.

I picked up the torch from him some years ago, in Colorado. The omens were inauspicious: I lost my first chance to hear that sweet "Sorry." As a corporate employee of a home-building firm, I'd finessed a job writing carpentry manuals just by suggesting to management that there was a need for clear explanation of our procedures.

One night, Pop had exciting news. "Son, I've got your first rejection. All you have to do is go down and pick it up." What a break. At my job, the only rejection slip I could get was a pink one.

Pop had wandered into an editor's office at the *Colorado Springs Sun*, hunting an annuity sale; but ink knows its own, and the editor mentioned that he was looking for someone to freelance a few local features. He suggested an Indian exposition south of town, and my father thought of me.

"Hell, you don't know a thing about features," he encouraged.

But the man in charge of the multi-tribal village was an ex-journalist. He practically guided me through the interview after I let on that this was my first story. The fact that Native-American lore is a hobby of mine didn't help. The piece came weirdly to life, and the *Sun* bought it. I was elated, but I was still at the starting gate.

"There'll be other stories," my father said with a shrug. "The journey of a thousand miles begins with the first step. Now get out there and blow one."

My enthusiasm betrayed me. I wrote about local events, trends, and people that fascinated me, and the editor apparently overlooked my occasional disqualifying grammatical error. I sold him my next three articles, and each one was a little smoother than the last.

My mentor was confident. "We'll get you started. Try a national magazine. Go right over the transom. You're in the nine hundreds after that."

As it happened, I had an idea for *The Mother Earth News*. I'm basically a carpenter, so I sent in fifteen hundred words of personal experience on renovating a burnt-out house. It seemed like an idea strange enough to flop, and they'd never published anything like it, even though each issue always has a piece on creative housing. After the fourth rewrite, it seemed adequately rough, and I stuck in some color slides of the project so it wouldn't look too obvious. A "get-serious" letter from them would look good in my shoebox.

They bought it.

"This is eerie," said my old man, frowning at the check. "Maybe there's a curse on what I told you. Set your sights a little lower. I think One Thousand is psyching you out. Try for five hundred for now, and the last five hundred will come easier."

If there was a curse, I could outrun it. I moved to Oregon, and sent in something to another national—and got my very first rejection slip. It was beautiful, a printed form addressed, "Dear Contributor." I had it framed. Two more rejections, and I was rolling.

My first effort for a regional weekly magazine seemed nicely unsuitable. It was about our wedding. Unfortunately, we were married in a covered bridge on Valentine's Day, and they liked it. "Thanks," they jeered.

Well, peachy, but you can't save a check. I tried again, struggling against acceptance, with a query on the Washington Stonehenge, a monument they'd beaten to death. But wouldn't you know it, we'd visited that fairy ring of stones during a witches' celebration of the summer solstice. The editor was looking for an arcane piece.

Determined not to take yes for an answer, I tried a humorous St. Patrick's Day tale called "How the Leprechauns Came to Oregon." And I sent it in early enough so they'd have time to consider something better. It was taking a chance, because St. Paddy's fell on Sunday, the day they published.

The deputy editor called up, chuckling: a bad sign. She slyly asked if it was a true story.

"It's a damn lie," I confessed, relieved. Another one in the shoebox.

"Ho-kay. Then we'll run it under a different head."

Last week, my father phoned. "How many so far?"

"Almost a pound," I side-stepped. One fifteenth done. Some torchbearer.

"You're better off not counting them. That was my mistake."

I told him about the leprechaun story. He snorted.

"Doomed to sell. Odd slant on a strong peg, and timed right."

"Slant? Peg?"

"Never mind. Send them a near-miss, and they'll turn you down as fast as anyone else." He paused. "Know what you're doing wrong? You target markets to suit your interests, and you memorize the listings in *Writer's Market*. You find unusual angles. You rewrite a story until it's smooth, but not slick from handling. And you read the publications first, for God's sake!"

"Every back issue I can get my hands on," I granted him.

"Well"—a long sigh—"I've done all I can. You have the forbidden knowledge that editors across the centuries have kept hidden from beginning freelancers. Just keep writing and submitting. Some things will sell, and some won't. The ones that won't, send out again. You might get ten turndowns from one idea."

"But what if they eventually sell?"

"That," he said firmly, "comes with the territory."

And so I write, when an idea comes to mind. Like everyone else, I have a collection of refusals. The shoebox overflowed one day, but I'm optimistic about the future—I use a trunk now. I'm still more than nine hundred get-lost cards away from being a successful writer. Above all, I never let an occasional sale discourage me. Because someday I'll open my mailbox and find that golden, final, liberating thousandth rejection slip. And the door to success will swing wide open.

A Writer's Prayer
by Lawrence Block

A common editor's prayer (at least for this editor) is that he will never again receive a submission titled "A Writer's Prayer." Aspiring contributors send me poems and essays and even letters to the editor thusly labeled by the pound (second only to articles about rejection—see previous article). So why did I allow this article, which originally appeared as an installment of Larry's monthly Fiction column for Writer's Digest, *to retain that hackneyed title?*

Well, it is indeed a prayer, not that the others so titled aren't. But this is a worthy prayer, an unselfish one, and one that deserves to be answered.

Lord, I hope You've got a few minutes. I've got a whole lot of favors to ask You.

Basically, Lord, I guess I want to ask You to help me be the best writer I possibly can, to get the most out of whatever talent I've been given. I could probably leave it at that, but I think it might help me to get a little more specific.

For starters, help me to avoid comparing myself to other writers. I can make a lot of trouble for myself when I do that, sliding into a routine that might go something like this:

"I'm a better writer than Alan, so why don't I have the success he has? Why don't I get book club sales? Why wasn't my last book optioned for a TV miniseries? How come Barry gets so much more advertising support from his publisher than I do? What's so great about Carol that she deserves a two-page review in *The New Yorker?* Every time I turn on the TV, there's Dan running his mouth on another talk show. What makes him so special? And how come Ellen's in *Redbook* four or five times a year? I write the same kind of story and mine keep coming back with form rejection slips.

"On the other hand, I will never be the writer Frank is. He can use his own experience with a degree of rigorous self-honesty that's beyond me. And Gloria has a real artist's eye. Her descriptive passages are so vivid they make me aware of my own limitations. Howard's a real pro—he can knock off more work in a day than I can in a month, and do it without working up a sweat. Irene spends twice as much time at the typewriter as I do. Maybe she has the right idea, and I'm so lazy I don't deserve to get any place at this game. And as for Jeremy. . . ."

Lord, let me remember that I'm not in competition with other writers. Whether they have more or less success has nothing to do with me. They have their stories to write and I have mine. The more I focus on comparing myself with them, the less energy I am able to concentrate on making the best of myself and my own work. I wind up despairing of my ability and bitter about its fruits, and all I manage to do is sabotage myself.

Help me, Lord, to write my own stories and novels. At the beginning I may have to spend a certain amount of time doing unwitting imitations of other people's work. That's because it may take me a while to find out what my own stories are and how to tap into them. But I'm sure they exist and I'm sure it will ultimately be possible for me to find them.

Flannery O'Connor said somewhere that anybody who manages to survive childhood has enough material to write fiction for a lifetime. I believe this, Lord. I believe every human being with the impulse to write fiction has, somewhere within him or her, innumerable stories to write. They may not bear any obvious resemblance to my own experiences. They may be set in a land I never visited or at a time I never lived. But if they're the stories I am meant to write they will derive from my observations and experience in a significant way. I will know the feelings, the perceptions, the reactions, for having lived them in some important way.

Of the traits likely to help me get in touch with these stories, perhaps the most important is honesty. Help me, Lord, to be as honest as I'm capable of being every time I sit down at the typewriter. I don't mean by this that I feel I ought to be writing nonfiction in fiction's clothing, that I think honesty entails telling stories as they actually happened in real life. Fiction, after all, is a pack of lies. But let my fiction have its own inner truth.

When a character of mine is talking, let me listen to him and write down what I hear. Let me describe him, not with phrases dimly recalled from other books, but as I perceive him.

It seems to me that a major element of writing honestly lies in respecting the reader. Please, Lord, don't ever let me hold my audience in contempt. Sometimes I find this a temptation, because by diminishing the reader I am less intimidated by the task of trying to engage his interest and hold his attention. But in the long run I cannot be disrespectful of my reader without my work suffering for it.

If I cannot write for a particular market without condemning that market's readers, perhaps I'm banging my head against the wrong wall. If I can't write juveniles without being patronizing to young readers, I'm not going to be proud of my work, nor am I going to perform it well. If I can't write confessions or gothics or mysteries or westerns because I think the product is categorically garbage or the people who read it are congenital idiots, I am not going to be good at it and I am not going to gain satisfaction from it. Let me write what I'm able to respect, and let me respect those people I hope will read it.

Lord, let me keep a dictionary within arm's length. When I'm not sure of the spelling of a word, let me look it up—not so much because a misspelled word is disastrous as because of a propensity of mine for substituting another word out of simple laziness. By the same token, let me use the dictionary when I'm uncertain of the precise meaning of a word I want to use.

But don't let me keep a really good dictionary on my desk, Lord. Let me reserve my Oxford Universal Dictionary for important matters. If I grabbed it every time I wanted to check the spelling of *exaggerate*, only to spend twenty minutes in the happy company of word derivations and obsolete usages and other lexicographical debris, I would never get any work done. A small, dull, pedestrian dictionary close at hand is sufficient.

Checking spelling and definitions requires a certain degree of humility, Lord, and that's a characteristic I could use more of. It's easy for me to run short of humility—which seems curious, given how much I have to be humble about. But it strikes me that writing demands such colossal (I just looked up *colossal*—thanks) arrogance that humility gets lost in the shuffle. It takes arrogance, doesn't it, to sit down at a typewriter making up stories out of the whole cloth and expecting total strangers to be caught up in them? I can think of little more arrogant than every artist's implicit assumption that his private fantasies and perceptions are worth another person's rapt attention.

Humility helps me keep myself in perspective. When my humility is in good order, both success and failure become easier to take. I'm able to recognize that the fate of empires does not hinge upon my work. I can see then that my writing will never be perfect, and that perfection is not a goal to which I can legitimately aspire. All I ever have to do is the best I can.

Please let me learn, Lord, to let it go at that. My capacity for arrogance and self-indulgence is balanced by an equally limitless capacity for self-deprecation. I can be awfully hard on myself, Lord, and it serves no purpose. If I turn out five pages a day, I tell myself that with a little extra effort I could have produced six or eight or ten. If I write a scene without researching a key element of it, I accuse myself of being slipshod; if I do the research, I beat up on myself for wasting time that could have been spent turning out finished copy. If I rewrite, I call it a waste of time, a process of washing garbage. If I don't rewrite, I call it laziness.

This self-abuse is counterproductive. Give me, Lord, the courage to get through life without it.

Help me, Lord, to grow as a writer. There are so many opportunities to do so, to gain in skills and knowledge just by practicing my craft and keeping my eyes open. Every book I read ought to teach me something I can use in my own writing, if I approach it with a willingness to learn. When I read a writer who does things better than I do, enable me to learn from him. When I read another writer who has serious weaknesses, allow me to learn from his mistakes.

Give me the courage to take chances. There was a point early in my career when I spent far too long writing inferior work, work that did not challenge me, that I could no longer respect, and that I no longer was able to grow from. I did this out of fear. I was afraid to take chances, either economically or artistically, afraid I might produce something unpublishable.

I have grown only when I have been willing to extend myself, to run risks. Sometimes I have failed, certainly, but help me to remember that I have always been able to learn from this sort of failure, that it has invariably redounded to my benefit in the long run. And, when I do take chances and do fail again, let me remember that so that the memory may soften the pain of failure.

Let me be open to experience, Lord, in life as well as at the typewriter. And give me the courage to take my experience undiluted, and to get through it all without chemical assistance. There was a time, Lord, when a little green pill in the morning seemed to concentrate my energies and improve my writing. It turned out that I was merely borrowing tomorrow's energy today, and the interest turned out to be extortionate in the extreme. There was a time, too, when other chemicals in pill or liquid form brought me what passed for relaxation. All of those props limited my capacity for experience and narrowed my vision like blinders on a horse. I thought I needed those things to write, Lord, and have since found out how much better I can write without them. They kept me from growing, from learning, from improving. Please help me keep away from them a day at a time.

Let me know, too, where my responsibilities as a writer begin and end. Help me to concentrate my efforts on those aspects of my career I can personally affect and let go of those over which I can have no control. Once I've put a manuscript in the mail, let me forget about it until it either comes back or finds a home. Let me take the appropriate action, Lord, without diluting my energies worrying over the result of that action. My primary job is writing. My secondary job is offering what I've written for sale. What happens after that is somebody else's job.

Don't let me forget, Lord, that acceptance and rejection aren't all that important anyway. The chief reward of any artistic effort (and perhaps of every other effort as well) is the work itself. Success lies in the accomplishment, not in its fruits. If I write well, I'm a success. Wealth and fame might be fun (or they might not), but they are largely beside the point.

Let me accept rejection, when it comes, as part of the process of gaining acceptance. Let me accept dry spells as part of the creative process. All across the board, Lord, let me accept the things I can't do anything about, deal with the things I can, and tell which is which.

And let me always be grateful, Lord, that I am a writer, that I am actually doing the only work I've ever really wanted to do, and that I don't need anyone's permission to do it. Just something to write with and something to write on.

Thanks for all that. And thanks for listening.

Blockbuster
by Barry B. Longyear

You'll meet Barry Longyear at greater length later on in this volume. For now, suffice it to say that Barry has found a couple of bedside requests that Larry Block didn't mention in his writer's prayer that you just finished reading (if, of course, you are reading the pieces in the order of their appearance).

Although I have been publishing professionally for seven years, with seven books and numerous short stories to my credit, the cursed writer's block has visited my workplace frequently. One block lasted longer than a year. However, since taking up the practice of reciting the following at the beginning of each writing day, writer's block and a heap of other miseries have left me.

God, grant me inspiration, relieve me of expectation, quiet that voice in me for which nothing is good enough.

When I research, lead me to the answers. When I plan, show me the path. When I write, allow me to enter and live my story. And when the story is done, clear it and its future from my mind.

If material success should come my way, remind me to thank You. However, if the only reward I obtain for my writing is the writing itself, let it be sufficient.

section four

"AUTHOR! AUTHOR!"
A Day in the Writing Life

A fan steps out of your shower. You meet an old friend not long after you've written a Broadway smash and he asks you if you're still working at the post office. Your husband comments to friends, "Have you ever smelled a writer on deadline?"

For a writer, just one of those days. . . .

Romancing the Drone
by Robyn Carr

I first met Robyn at a writers conference in Sacramento. I was one of the speakers, and she was one of the people working together to stage the event. Robyn showed me then, and has showed me over and over since, that she is bright and witty, and outspoken—she'd be the first to point out the triteness of my phrase, "bright and witty."

Robyn is also one of the most perceptive writers I have ever met. She once wrote an article for us called "Are You a Writer?" In it, she asked a series of questions, and readers could earn 0-3 points for each answer. When it came time to total the score, Robyn wrote: "If you're still trying to calculate a score, try a career in computer science where definite questions have definite answers. In writing, you 'feel' a lot more than you 'compute.' You have what it takes to be a writer if the schizophrenic quality of the questions and answers frustrated yet intrigued you. Writing is a roller-coaster ride with ups and downs and sharp turns. You get to keep guessing what's going to happen next, to continue digesting information from periodicals, groups, critiques, conferences, books that have 'made it,' author interviews, etc.—and to keep learning. After all this, if you're still writing, you're a writer."

This tale shows Robyn putting that practical attitude to day-to-day use.

There is not a romance writer in America who did not identify with Kathleen Turner's role as a romance writer when watching *Romancing the Stone*. Like Turner's Joan Wilder, most of us, by the end of the novel we're writing, don't have any supplies left in the house, smell like a soldier returning from battle, can't find anyone but the cat to share our celebration, and if we were sent to South America, we would end up on the wrong bus. The part about Michael Douglas was pure fiction.

The results of an interesting survey recently surfaced. Researchers interviewed a cross section of women and discovered that those who read sexy romance novels make love 74 percent more often than those who don't read them. This is going to be great for marketing. The romance book display at your local bookseller might be moved into the "Lifestyles" or "Self-Improvement" section. I will not comment on the billing.

But what of the women who write them? The researchers did not plan this, I'm sure, but the results of the survey were released at the time of a huge convention of romance writers, readers, publishers, and others in New York City. Many of us brought our husbands. We did our own survey. It is possible that the novelists themselves enjoy a life of romance someplace beneath the readers of *Field & Stream*.

"Is it the commitment and overpowering concentration required to write a book?" an editor asked the spouse of a romance writer.

"No," he replied, scratching his chin and pondering. "I think it's probably the sweat pants."

"Surely," another person offered, "the intensity of involvement in a major writing project is so consuming that there is too little energy left."

"Do you know what ten years on a desk chair does to the gluteus maximus?" the husband replied.

"Have you ever *smelled* a writer on deadline?" another asked.

"Have you ever *heard* a writer who hasn't had one good idea in a week?"

Perhaps there are some illusions about the private lives of these women who write the spicy, dicy, sexy romances. Perhaps the personal benefits from reading them are quite different from the side effects of writing them. I don't want to suggest that we are not a romantic bunch. By gosh, we sure are. In fact, I had a romantic evening with my husband not too long ago that was refreshingly spontaneous. He came home after a four-day trip, exhausted and smelling like the cockpit of an airplane. I was in the kitchen trying to piece together a dinner after a long day of typing. I was experiencing a slight time warp. The children were having a twentieth-century fight while my head still buzzed with a fourteenth-century joust. When a tired and hungry pilot walked in, it threw me. We didn't exactly embrace like long-lost lovers, but we did try our hand at conversation. But, these prepubescent creatures we live with were shrieking and it was already too late to guess who had started it. We would not be denied the warmth and intimacy of our reunion, so we grabbed a bottle of jug-wine from the refrigerator and hid in the Volkswagen in the driveway. We didn't go back to the kitchen until enough time had elapsed for the fighting barbarians to either have it settled or do each other in. That might not make good copy, but if it isn't true love, I don't know what is.

The greatest thing I've found in ten years of meeting with the writers of romances is how regular their lives are. I just received a letter from a friend who has published about a dozen books. It wasn't really a letter; it was an excuse. She said she was between deadlines and had to scoop out the house, find out where her children were living, call her husband's secretary and ask if he was still with the same company, pay her library fines, and then she would write me a letter.

Another writer friend, one who is famous and enormously successful, wrote that Christmas was past, deadline was fast approaching, and she was getting out the peach brandy and electric blanket for the long haul ahead. I think she pays for housekeeping, but I'm not going to ask. Obviously, the only difference between awesome success and moderate success for romance writers is what you drink at the end of the line and whether you can plug in the blanket you slump under when it's over. Writing takes just about everything you've got whether you're rich or poor.

I'm sure that we could do many things to spice up our personal lives. And who better? These are the creative minds that put women in fetching gowns, men in impeccable suits, and passion at the right place and time. This romance writer is married to a man who would like to keep some of the illusions alive; he would like to see me perform a Loretta Young swirl into the family room after a day of dredging my brain for one good paragraph. He keeps trying to trick me into it. Once I complained that the hardest part of my job is getting myself into my office to start writing. I always find something that has to be done first.

An evil glitter came into his eye. He saw his chance. (He was one of the spouses who mentioned sweat pants.) "Here's what you do," he said. "You set a time to be at the office. You get up, shower, fix your hair, put on your make-up, pantyhose. . . ."

"Pantyhose?" I choked, afraid.

"Now, if you want this to work, pantyhose. And then you get in the car, drive around the block, enter your place of business, and just like the rest of us, no matter what you see or hear on the way to your office, you have to get to work on time."

"In my pantyhose and make-up?"

"It's all part of creating the scenario that puts you in a working frame of mind."

I thought about it for a minute. "Nice try" was all I said.

And why is it always up to the women to make the relationships romantic? This advice about wearing make-up to my place of business (which is down the hall, one giant step over the laundry hamper, sharp right at the fingerprints on the wall) comes from a man who spends every weekend in the same pair of jogging shorts with a dead elastic waistband and will shave on a Saturday only if we're trying to sell our house. This is the male romantic lead. I should type in taffeta?

I'm not going to argue that the writing life doesn't hold some element of glamour. I can be as glamorous as the next person. In fact, when I attended the extravaganza of romantic writers, we all looked wonderful. Everything from handsome business suits to fancy dresses, chic hair crops to curly tresses, plucked brows, polished nails, poise and charisma. But none of the writers got there by looking beautiful or being fascinating. They got there by never having time to read the mail addressed to "occupant," spending hours chewing erasers off pencils in search of ideas, and futilely attempting to staple the pages back into their thesauruses. By the fifth day, all still looking great, mutterings started to rise from the crowd. "Shoes. Who ever heard of such a thing?" "My nail fell off and she swore it would hold through the autograph session." "Is it whiteout that stops a run? I forgot." No matter how high we go, we all started in the same place.

Everybody knows, deep down, that a tremendous sense of commitment and hard, hard work is required to emerge successful in any profession. In writing, well, there's no time clock, minimum wage, or dress code, and our co-workers are usually telephone acquaintances. What we look like on the job may not make *Cosmopolitan*. I think I can speak for most other romance writers when I say we were gratified to learn that women who read our stuff are getting a lot out of it. (So to speak.)

Some of us are starting a campaign to get our husbands to read what we write, since the books are credited with putting sizzle into the old marriage. One friend of mine had a T-shirt made for her spouse that says "Research Assistant." It created something of a problem when he read her book. "Where do you *get* those ideas?" he asked.

Another friend was telling me that a reporter asked her if her books were, in any way, fashioned after some of her own personal experiences. "Can you imagine," she said with a laugh, "if the biggest problems I had were how to wake in the morning and stretch with feline grace, and how I would get my tremendous bosom into my ballgown?"

"What did you say?" we all demanded in unison.

"I said, 'Yes.' "

There are two definitions for *steamy*, and one of them has to do with ironing. The other steam comes off the keyboard and settles onto the pages, and apparently we're doing our jobs well because they're still selling like hotcakes. But does it follow that if women who read romances have more romantic lives, women who read horror stories commit more heinous crimes? Or are we just all different people who live different lives?

The little group of romance writers I meet with regularly discussed the survey. I can vouch for the fact that we were all inspired. One writer threatened to stop writing romances so she could read more. Another said she was making plans to move to the city where the survey had been conducted. Mostly we decided that we preferred life in the trenches, that our work was as much fun as our fantasies, and that if our lives weren't totally romantic it was our husbands' fault.

We have come out of the ether, we decided together. Following is a list of realities that keep us sane and keep us working hard to please our readers:

A. *There is always one more romantic conflict that we'd rather write about than have.*

B. *A romance writer's clothing line would not make* Glamour.

C. *The part about Michael Douglas was pure fiction.*

King of the Road
by Larry L. King

*Larry L. King is, as of this writing, the author of eleven
books, including* None But a Blockhead: On Being a Writer; *of three plays, including* The Best Little Whorehouse in
Texas; *and of hundreds of magazine articles, which have
appeared in publications ranging from* Life *to* Parade *to*
Atlantic Monthly. *These credits are good enough to allow
him to be cocky if he wanted to be. And maybe he does
want to be—I don't know—but I do know that he's not.
As he wrote in "Somewhere Between a Busboy and a Rodeo Clown . . . and Too Proud to Seek Honest Work,"
published in our* Writer's Yearbook: *"The night I called
Texas, in 1972, to spread the joyous news that my* Confessions of a White Racist *had been nominated for a National
Book Award (against, I explained, the offerings of such literary heavyweights as Norman Mailer, Mike Royko, and
Tom Wolfe), Mama patiently heard me out and then said,
'But, Son, why don't you settle down and see if you can
find something steady?' "*

Writers often are subjected to a peculiar ritual known as The
Promotional Tour. Those who never have experienced such a tour
probably consider it a wonderful opportunity to advertise one's
work and one's self. There is this fantasy of being so charming and
erudite that Johnny Carson will kidnap you for post-show drinks,
and of common citizens offering a standing ovation should you enter a lunch room. In truth, The Promotional Tour can be as painful
as a car wreck and as humbling as the public pratfall.

Newspaper people who interview the touring writer usually
have read his or her book. Radio interviewers *may* have. Television
folk—well, I here offer a cash reward to anyone who can prove beyond doubt that any television interviewer, anywhere in the world,
has ever read any book whatsoever. Those "television personalities," with their smooth plastic faces, capped teeth, and blow-dry
hair—whether boys or girls—are likely to turn your book in their
hands as if they suspect it might explode, smile brightly when the
camera lights flick on, and say, "Tell us all about your new book,

Mr. Green." This is particularly disconcerting if your name is not Green. Even if it is, have you ever tried summarizing a book—*any* book—in a seven-minute monologue while your interviewer yawns, sneaks looks at his or her watch, jots postcards home, or waves to pals in the control room?

The writer may also wish for better placement on talk shows. One prays to come on behind a comedian or song stylist who has put the studio audience and the one at home in an upbeat mood. I have had to follow such tough acts as 1) a stuttering gynecologist who, with the aid of color charts, came out against cancer of the uterus; 2) a grim government official who professed that nuclear war might not be all bad if only one could keep the proper perspective; and 3) an eleven-year-old horseshoe-pitching champion who, attempting to give an exhibition of his winning form, proved on that day to be unable to hit the side of a barn with a sack full of BBs. Just as I was introduced, he broke down and cried. Very shortly thereafter, so did I.

Beware the highly publicized autograph session at bookstores. It is terribly embarrassing to sit behind a tall stack of your own books for two hours while customers sidestep your table, throwing sneaky or hostile glances, en route to selecting an armful of cookbooks, diet books, and how-to books written by total strangers. I have learned that it is not considered good form to curse or threaten them. On one occasion, in my hometown of Midland, Texas, I suffered in silence for the better part of a hot afternoon when absolutely *no* customers came into the bookstore—until, suddenly, I saw the face of an old high school chum not glimpsed in twenty years. Wellsir, I hugged him and called him by name and waltzed him around, thanking him for the high honor of his visit. He looked a bit perplexed, bashfully dug his toe into the floor, and said, "Hail, Larry, they just called me over here to fix the cigarette machine."

Hometowns have a way of putting us back in touch with reality. Shortly after the cigarette machine incident—following local interviews and having my name in lights on the sign in front of the Holiday Inn—I was strutting to coffee with the town mayor, feeling so Famous that I wondered why someone wasn't running ahead to scatter rose petals in my path, when I saw another old friend coming down the street. "Tommy!" I greeted him, opening my arms wide to receive his accolades for having made good in the big literary world. He tossed me a casual wave and said, "Hi, Larry, you still workin' over at the post office?"

Though publishing houses and their publicity people insist

that Promotional Tours increase the sales of all books subjected to the ritual, I occasionally have moments of doubt. Viking Press once dispatched me on a twenty-eight-day, thirty-three-city romp that included many major TV shows—among them *Today,* Dick Cavett, *Kup's Show* in Chicago, David Susskind—and after all that work, talk and travel, the highly touted book in question sold a mere seven thousand hardcover copies. I later groused to Viking's publicity chief that, given the book's great reviews, it would have sold that many had I been content to hawk it from my front stoop. She looked down her nose as if sniffing something slightly malodorous and said coldly, "Perhaps we'll let you prove that when and *if* your next book is published." I rushed to send her three dozen American Beauty roses and a mash note, just in case my promotional theories happened to be wrong.

The fact is, nobody knows why some books go through the roof beginning the day they come from the bindery, or why others cannot be sold if hustled coast to coast with the help of champagne and dancing girls—though, somehow, I think it helps if the author's name is Irving. Uncertainties of formula add spice and zest to the author's life, and probably account for that fat, bearded, pale man you saw crying on the bus this morning.

Not Sleeping with Steinbeck

by Linda Belknap

Many writers dream of their bylines appearing in such magazines as Glamour. *Linda Belknap never had such a dream. She could never fall asleep long enough to get the dream started in the first place. So, eyes as wide and bright as the moon that shone at that time of the night, she wrote the articles that allowed her to get her byline into* Glamour *and other publications. And she wrote this. . . .*

Three A.M. House quiet as a Q-tip. Son sleeping. (Sure. He's a child.) Ditto husband. (Sure. He's a psychologist.) Once again I fall suddenly, inexplicably, awake. My leg twitches. My mind leaps. My eyes sting. Hooray, I whisper. It's time to ease on my night light, muffle my ballpoint, and write.

I am a writer. I am an insomniac. I am a writer hyphen insomniac the way other people are actor hyphen directors or clerk hyphen typists. One talent feeds the other. It's not as good as being bilingual or even ambidextrous, but it's what I do best.

Now, most folks do not feel this way about wakefulness. Among the general public, getting the proverbial good night's sleep has become a national obsession. Despite all evidence to the contrary, the eight-hour snooze is believed to be mandatory, a duty, a civil liberty protected by the Constitution and upheld in court.

An estimated 20-35 million Americans consider themselves insomniacs. This is a lot of people sporting black sateen eyeshades and breathing out of alternate nostrils, all because they heard that humans should spend a third of their lives sleeping. And the potential cures don't stop there. Progressive relaxation. Autogenic training. Adjustable beds. Raw onions on toast. The list is, well, exhaustive. Just reading it could be the best soporific of all.

The thing is, I enjoyed insomnia for years before I found out it was bad. I still haven't broken the news to my mother, who wastes part of every night reading classics, eating ice cream, and writing letters to *her* mother, who doesn't sleep a "normal" night either.

At first, the wakefulness seemed to coincide with my coming of age and taking on the problems of the world. Suddenly I was lying awake in August debating what to get Great Aunt Edith for Christmas. My notebook from that period reveals: "Fruit basket?" Then, in a firmer hand, "Scarf."

As I started composing more than shopping lists, my night notes took a decidedly literary turn. Phrases I had argued with all morning now stepped meekly into place. From some hidden reservoir flowed article ideas, chapter headings, market strategies, and book titles so brilliant that I dare not disclose them here. (Well, OK. Just one. My own contribution to the occupational series. *So You Want to Be a . . . Clamdigger.*)

About a year ago, into this ocean of inspiration came the nagging thought that nighttime was dark for a reason, the reason *not* being so K-Mart could sell pen-size flashlights. But it was too late. By now I was sleeping a split shift because I needed to. I craved those peaceful pre-dawn hours with the world to myself. I was intrigued by the mysterious subconscious process. Besides, I hadn't yet written one word of *Clamdigger.*

Imagine, then, my delight at stumbling across an entry made by John Steinbeck in *Journal of a Novel.* "Last night I hardly slept at all," wrote Steinbeck, adding, "It was one of those good thinking nights."

A good thinking night? Did I detect a positive attitude toward some extra hours of wakefulness? I did. Not only did Steinbeck not worry about insomnia, but he also actually seemed to welcome it. The plot of *East of Eden* evolved in that twilight zone between midnight and morning when an ordinary insomniac would be watching the minute hand move on the lighted clock dial. This discovery fired me to make even better use of the gift of time. I resolved that, minimally, I would be up addressing envelopes. In time, perhaps I'd be not-sleeping almost as well as John.

To test my newly opened eyes, I glanced through *How to Get a Good Night's Sleep,* by Richard Trubo. I'm proud to say I wasn't even tempted by a hint that I could court sleep by eating creamed cottage cheese. Instead, I was gratified to learn that other famous writers were also strange bedfellows, although somewhat less cheerfully than Steinbeck.

Rudyard Kipling is said to have lamented: "Pity us! Oh, pity us! We wakeful." Charles Dickens grew weary of "always tossing about like a distressed ship in a sea of bedclothes." Twain, Poe, and Proust were all insomniacs to one degree or another, according to

Trubo. A last bit of inadvertent research clinched my case. Rereading *The Snake Has All the Lines,* I found Jean Kerr's "nocturnal doodlings," these being letters of protest she had the good sense not to mail.

Someday scientists may have time to measure the correlation between insomnia and specific careers. So far, they have been pretty busy thinking up words like *initardia, scurzomnia,* and *hyperlixia* to describe the various sleep disorders. Until writing and its accompanying insomnia are proven to be hazardous to one's health, the following observations will have to do. (Bear with me. I got an A in Logic 101.)

1. According to a Stanford University Medical Center study, most sleep disturbances are caused by fears and emotional anxieties.

2. After researching the health of authors for his Lloyd Roberts Lecture, Harold Nicolson concluded that all creative writers are hypochondriacs since they are always worrying about either their bodies or their minds.

3. Nicolson further noted that writers, especially poets, object to being thought "normal." Thus, they are eager to display eccentricities.

4. Some psychologists say that if an insomniac enjoys any special status due to the condition, motivation to sleep well will be lacking.

5. Heaven knows people are impressed with the notion of Creative Thoughts striking a writer down mid-slumber. The amount of admiration reaped in this fashion is directly proportionate to the number of one's bestselling novels snapped up by the book clubs in the last six months.

6. While insomnia may be on the rise, accepting insomnia isn't.

7. Therefore, the new frontier for the creative, eccentric, insecure, insomniac writer may well be wearing his or her wakefulness with a smile.

True insomnia is sometimes defined as a chronic affliction that keeps the sufferer from functioning normally the next day. Since I have already shown that writers are rarely, indeed prefer not to be, normal, I may never know if my sleeplessness is fact or fiction.

No matter. It serves my purpose. I will endure it, enjoy it, invite it. In fact, I will follow the lead of Brian Aldiss, who waxed poetic about dawn and cloud cover. And Ogden Nash, who waxed hilarious about artificial sleep aids such as yawn plaques and slumber buzzers.

Tonight, when I wake up, I will start my new book. Luckily, I already have a brilliant title. I'm calling it, *So You Want to Be an . . . Insomniac.*

I Used to Be Taller
by Crying Wind

*Halfway between Possum Flats and Cow Skin lives Crying
Wind, the author of the books* When I Give My Heart,
Crying Wind, *and* My Searching Heart, *and of more than
two hundred short stories, with her husband and four children. You'll understand why I'm not any more precise
about her location when you read her gentle complaints
that are about to follow.*

*I thought that maybe the rattlesnake farm she mentions
here was a joke, until I received a letter from her recently:
"Last night I discovered a three-foot copperhead snake in
my office (it looked thirty feet long, but I'm trying to be
honest). I figured it was either an anonymous gift from an
ex-fan, an omen from God that I should give up writing,
or a sign that I should keep my office door tightly closed."*

*And maybe I should add that Crying Wind just ran out
of coffee. . . .*

"Who in the devil was that?" my husband gasped when a man
wearing only a bathrobe walked through our kitchen and disappeared into the bathroom.

"I don't have the slightest idea," I said as I buttered my toast.
"But the rest of his family are setting up their camper in our front
yard."

"But who are they?" Don demanded. His voice had risen a full
octave.

"Remember when I spoke at that convention in Detroit last
winter and ended my speech by saying, 'If you're ever in my neighborhood, stop in for coffee'? Well, that lady outside is here for her
cup of coffee."

"But who is in my shower?"

"I think it's her husband."

"But there were *six thousand* people at that convention!" His
voice was trembling. "Which one is she?"

"She said I would remember her because she was the lady in the
blue suit who sat in the second row."

My husband reached for the bottle of aspirin. He was too late.

I had just popped the last one into my mouth.

It was going to be a long summer.

I had thought that it was friendly to invite people to stop in for coffee—and safe to do so, because we lived in the Colorado Rockies fifty miles from the nearest town. Yet, that summer more than 150 people found their way to our door and collected not only the cup of coffee but also flowers from our garden, shrubs from our yard, and endless snapshots of our family posing with Aunt Mabel and Uncle Charlie. One group of fans claimed to have engine trouble. They parked their camper in our yard for three days while they borrowed bread and milk, used our shower, and asked me to "just wash up a few little things for them." While their dirty underwear was tumbling around in my washer, I wondered why I hadn't thrown them off the property. The only answer I could come up with was that they were fans, they had bought six copies of each of my books, and they would continue to buy my future books after they returned to Michigan.

People trailed in and out of our lives that summer, often arriving at mealtime, wanting to visit for "just a minute" (it was never just a minute). They took pictures, asked me to sign books (and add something personal) while my dinner got cold and soggy. I smiled until my jaw ached and listened to their comments about my home, my books, and frequently, my photograph on my book jacket. People mentioned that I looked taller in my pictures so many times that I gave up explaining camera angles. "You're right," I would say. "I used to be taller."

To add to the confusion, I received twenty to thirty calls a day—most of them beginning, "You don't know me, but I read your books and. . . ."

We changed our private phone number three times—only to find out a friend was selling our phone number for five dollars a whack.

My husband saved our sanity when he bought a phone-answering machine. Next to my typewriter, it's the best thing I own. The tape on the machine tells everyone that I'm working on a new novel (when I'm really cleaning the bathtub) and asks the caller to leave a message. Within two months, my calls had dropped to a glorious average of two a day. Heaven!

And even seemingly harmless newspaper interviews got me in trouble. One story announced I was flying to Chicago the next day to appear on a television talk show. Our house was burglarized while I was gone. The thief even stole the meat from the freezer.

In a desperate attempt to regain some privacy, I erected two signs. One read, WARNING! I SHOOT EVERY THIRD VISITOR. THE SECOND VISITOR JUST LEFT! We respect your privacy—please respect ours.

In case that didn't discourage intruders, a second sign read, RATTLESNAKE VENOM FARM . . . DO NOT LEAVE YOUR CAR. NOT RESPONSIBLE FOR ACCIDENTS.

Nearly every day we would see fresh tracks of cars that had made it as far as the rattlesnake sign before they turned around and left.

Don't get me wrong. I really do appreciate each person who buys one of my books; I would be nothing without my readers. But the very fans who love your books are the ones who will monopolize your time and energy and prevent you from writing.

I'm now experienced enough and tough enough to say to myself that I owe my fans only a good story for their money. They aren't buying a visit to my home, or a picture of me with Aunt Mabel, or a look into my private life. When I'm on tour, I'm happy to sign books, pose for pictures, and have coffee with them if I can fit it into my schedule, but when I'm home, I want my private life to stay private.

I can finally say "No."

In fact, just this morning I told Don: "At least mail is a cinch. I used to feel morally responsible to answer each and every letter. Now, except for a few very special letters, I only answer the ones that contain a stamped, self-addressed envelope." He nodded and smiled.

I even kept my resolve when I read a desperate letter from Alma, a woman in her late sixties, who assured me she was honest, respectable, and sane. However, when her literary club had reviewed my book, "that Sarah Trimble, the Old Biddy," had bragged about how she was going to mail her book to the author and ask her to autograph it. For some reason, Alma had told Sarah Trimble that she'd be most happy to get an autograph for Sarah, because Alma was one of my closest friends. When the group's attention was suddenly focused on her, Alma threw caution to the wind and said she was, in fact, having lunch with me on Friday. The club president, Sarah Trimble and Alma's closest friend, begged to come along and Alma was trapped. Her letter pleaded with me to meet her and the other ladies at a certain restaurant in town at noon Friday, and to pretend to be a friend of hers. I would recognize Alma because she would wear a pink lace dress with a string of pearls. If I didn't show up (and she wouldn't blame me at all if I didn't) she would confess all. She would never be able to show her face at the literary club again. But the worst part, she wrote, would be letting Sarah Trimble, That Old Biddy, get the last laugh.

I looked at Don, smiled coldly, set my jaw like Clint Eastwood and laughed. "Aha! Another cheap trick! A month ago, this might have worked, but now I'm in control of my life. People will no longer take advantage of me!"

"What are you going to do?"

"There is just one way to handle this lady . . . I will meet her at noon on Friday and pretend to be a close dear friend. I will be charming and cheerful and make the lady in the pink lace dress feel like the best friend I've ever had. After all, I've known a few Sarah Trimbles in my life."

My husband shook his head as I tucked the letter into my pocket. But this was a job I couldn't refuse. How often do you get to feel like the Lone Ranger riding to the rescue?

Author! Author!
by Juli Tarpin

How easy for Juli to write this piece. It was all in her note-books, after all . . .
   Well, maybe it was easy, and maybe it wasn't. I can only say for sure that reading it is easy . . . and fun . . . and full of dots . . .

All my life I have yearned to write . . . you know . . . The Great American novel. Ever since I was a little girl I have toted this dream around with me, carried it everywhere, much as a kangaroo carries her young. It has sustained me through some perilous times—(take, as one example, the time I scorched, not one, but *two* of my husband's favorite shirts)—this hope that someday I would write a very . . . *stylistic* book: a sort of long, surreal, prose *poem*, perhaps, or maybe a narcissistic stream-of-consciousness narrative filled with lilting, lucid sentences containing marvelous adjectives culled from *Roget's Thesaurus*, and embroidered here and there with *italics*, and . . . dots following the last word in each chapter. . . .
   (I'm daft about dots. . . .)
   Ah, was not the circumstance of a scorched shirt sleeve or two diminished to a mere trifle by the magnificent dimensions of a book such as mine would be?
   When I was ten years old, I did, in fact, type a fifty-odd-page book under the auspices of my father (who generously supplied me with a box of misprinted company letterhead), whose reluctant secretary I was, and in whose shoe factory my brother and I were pressed into service at an unbelievably tender age.
   Would you believe two little tots standing on chairs at midnight, sucking on lollipops and latexing innersoles for a rush Easter order for Kennedy's Shoe Stores? ("Two nimble-fingered, keen-eyed kids equal one uninspired adult laborer," my father muttered to my protesting mother. "Plus there's no payroll involved.")
   I titled my book *Four Sisters:* it was a blatantly plagiarized adaptation of Louisa May Alcott's *Little Women*, in which I was totally immersed at the time. Blissfully unaware of any trespass I was committing against my beloved authoress, I unhesitatingly named my heroines Amy, Beth, Jo, and Meg.

I wept as I typed a chapter in which Jo falls out of the third-floor window of her blind father's shoe factory the same day Meg (whose job it was to clean house while her mother worked to help meet the payroll for the factory) is electrocuted as she scrubs the inside of a light socket with creolin disinfectant.

I sobbed as Amy fights a losing battle with Dread Plague (contracted from her daily exposure to rubber latex cement), and who, despite this handicap, nurses her sister Beth (who has lost both arms to an eyelet machine) through a long convalescence:

"O, Amy! Amy!" Beth cried, wringing her feet (since she had no hands). "Whatever are we going to do?!"

"Be brave, Beth! Here! Try to hold this fork with your toes!"

I kept the manuscript under my mattress along with the confession pulps I had discovered in a variety store for a penny apiece with their covers torn off—a discovery that catapulted me upon a delightful, albeit dangerous detour from the yellow brick road of children's literature I had heretofore traveled—and in whose torrid pages I found titillating titles like: "I MARRIED A TWIN . . . and Discovered After Our Wedding Night That I Had Married My Brother-in-Law!", and pulse-pounding paragraphs beside which Alcott's tepid prose now palled.

My mother, puzzled as to why my mattress resembled the Himalayas found (and promptly confiscated) my entire magazine collection, including my typescript—(at the time she couldn't read, nor could she speak a word of English, but the pictures in the pulps that consisted, in the main, of scantily clad ladies lounging on unmade beds, provoked her into an hour-long harangue in her native tongue directed to me and my unfortunate choice of reading material)—and I watched, dry-eyed, as she stuffed the pages of *Four Sisters,* the last remnant of my innocent childhood, into the kitchen stove.

No matter! Relieved that I was no longer custodian of a manuscript that now seemed juvenile juxtaposed against a sophisticated story such as "I MARRIED THE DEVIL . . . He Made Me Sleep in a Coffin!", I grabbed my jump rope and went out to skip around the block, confident that I would, one day, write another book.

The *form* of my book was always vivid in my mind's eye. The first letter of the first word in each chapter would be giant Old English script, with ivy and flowers entwined around it. Yes!

No! Art Deco type! Spare. *Sans serif!* Like the print in that movie ad about Jean Harlow. Precisely!

After my shotgun marriage in 1946 (truth is, my father *was* at the point of shooting my then-fiance because he delivered me home from a ... ah ... date at 3 A.M. once too often) I bought yet another thick notebook with lots of pristine pages ...

... and wrote in it, even as tapioca pudding boiled over on the stove: *For quick sour milk, add 1 T vinegar to 1 cup fresh milk and let stand 10 minutes.*

I spent about twenty years on the dedication page. It changed, yearly. Safety pins in my mouth, powdering babies' bottoms, I would plot the latest version in my head. Without this literary diversion, how ever would I have survived my three *enfants terribles:* one who held her breath for a year (or so it seemed), one who didn't sleep a wink for two years, and one who subsisted solely on Ritz cracker crumbs and Kool-Aid for three years.

So much for domesticity and its dreary backdrop against which I played my supporting role of frustrated authoress. *OCCU-PATION: Writer* (I wrote, once) as the census taker cast a slitted eye at my protruding abdomen and the screaming moppet in the high-chair I had produced in lieu of a novel, fourteen months before ...

"Oh? What have you written?" she murmured, stooping to retrieve a dropped pencil from a puddle of lime Jell-O on the floor.

"You know those poems by 'Anonymous' in the paperback anthologies?" I hissed. "*Me!*"

And haughtily showed her the door.

One year, I wrote, cryptically: *To W. W. B., my first editor— because.*

And crossed it out—QUICK!

My gawd! What would people *think?!* ("Because of ... *what?!* So *that's* how she broke into print!")

To Linda, Carol, and Susan—my wonderful daughters who were a constant source of inspiration, and whose faith in me made this book possible.

Scene

Me: Honey, do you have a minute?

Any Daughter: Well ... *half* a minute. Why?

Me: Would you ... ah ... read this draft? It's only three pages, and. ...

Any Daughter: Ma, come *on!* I have to wash my *hair!*

Me (sniffing): Never mind. Forget it. Sorry I asked.

Any Daughter: You read it, OK? I'll listen. But hurry up! My hair is so gooey, I can't *stand* it!

Every year, the months sort of fell out of calendars. Drifted to the floor like leaves before a hurricane. One minute, it was 1946, and the next minute was 1981, which, as anyone with any sense of time running out *knows*, is practically 1984.

Desperate, now, I started counting pages in books. Three hundred pages is a book. OK! If I typed one page a day . . . *one page!* . . . I'd have a manuscript in . . . a year!

The mother of the bride wore an apricot gown of pleated chiffon. . . .

(That's what I wrote last year.)

All those years, I kept diaries filled with minutiae which, if compared to Samuel Pepys's journals in terms of output alone, would reduce his work to a mere jotting. I have thirty-four (count 'em! thirty-four!) of those page-a-day, hardbound daily-aides you buy in the 5&10 each January. The pages are splattered with Rorschach-type blots of . . . baby food, tomato sauce, mustard—an incredible palette attesting to the impossible conditions under which I attempted to record my life.

Would you believe I spent thirty-four years on *titles*?

Ms. Odalisque's Revenge! Revenge for what, or on who (whom?) I have never quite figured out, but it's a real winner title that keeps coming back, like a dream.

Only last week, I found, scribbled on the back of my paycheck stub:

Love's Last Lust
Lust's Last Love
Love's Last Love 2

And a long, convoluted column of penciled figures that give me a net of $1,000,000 for the paperback rights *alone!*

I've never ceased to marvel at how someone like, say, Rosemary Rogers *does* it. I was making French bread the day it was announced on the radio that her newest, *The Crowd Pleasers*, was rolling off the presses, and cleaning the oven when *Love Play* was announced on TV.

(Would you believe an effigy constructed of dough and shaped like a typewriter with the key section all pushed in?)

I went up to the attic the other day. Thumbed through some of the thirty-four slim volumes—a veritable *Encyclopaedia Britannica*—stacked on the floor between a shoebox of once-melted, fused-together crayons and a folded-up playpen.

(1948) Linda Juli born. 6 lbs. 7 oz. She's beautiful!

(1960) We moved into our new house today! The girls ecstatic because they have their own rooms, yet Suzi says she misses her sisters—two rooms away, down the hall! (And then, in a hand so fine and small, the words seem to be kneeling): O God, *please bless this home!*

(1980) Carol's wedding incredible! My last little sparrow has flown the nest. . . .

Scene

Me (sniffing): Not bad. Despite a tendency to sticky sentimentality—good, terse prose that moves right along. Real winner page turners, these.

And, downstairs, a burning smell, wafting up the attic stairs—potatoes burning dry—which penetrated only the very outermost edges of my consciousness, as I kept reading my ... ah ... books. . . .
(In truth—I couldn't put them down.)

section five

"MY NEW OLD TYPEWRITER"

Tales of Intimacies Unknown by Lovers—Writers and Their Writing Tools

Every profession has its symbols. For my wife the pharmacist, for instance, a mortar and pestle. For me the writer, the pen (quill, if I were a poet), or the typewriter (and now the word processor). Let me tell you, though, that few professions cling to their symbols the way writing does.

That's because our symbols are working symbols. My wife only occasionally uses a mortar and pestle at work. I'm never without a pen or pencil nearby. Almost never, anyway.

And I'm certain that my wife doesn't have a rela-

tionship with her mortar and pestle. But the writers included in this section do have relationships. They look odd to outsiders, but to other writers, they're quite normal.

Referential Treatment
by Martha Moffett

Have you ever tried to throw away a book?
  Such an action often has elements in common with dis-owning a child, filing for divorce, or shunning a friend. Books to writers are more partners than tools, because they physically represent the very stuff of our goals. Books result from the distilled genius and pained work of people who are very much like us, because they too are writers.
  And that's part of the heart of this article, written by a former editor who says that her work as a copy editor on The American Heritage Dictionary of the English Language *has left her with a serious addiction to semicolons; who can argue with her? In fact, I'm confident that Martha's tale will make* this volume *all the more difficult to throw away. . . .*

"Ma! Can you help me with my homework?"
  I look up from my typewriter. My fifteen-year-old, in her jeans and Fox shirt, is in the process of changing styles from preppy to surfer. Moving up, she calls it.
  "What is your homework?"
  "I have to make a list of reference books."
  "That should be easy," I say. "Let's see, there's your dictionary and atlas and almanac." I stop and look around our small house. It is crammed with books. And the attached garage is so full of books that I wouldn't be able to shelter the car there even if a hurricane threatened. "Actually," I begin again, broadening my guidelines, "almost any book is a reference book. A *cookbook* is a reference book."
  "I only need to list six," she says. This is my youngest child, who has learned to judge minimum requirements to a nicety, and be-lieves that this talent will get her through high school and later through college. Independent studies and extra-credit projects are not for her. As a result, she has much time to spend as she likes. I'm glad, really, that I have not passed my compulsions on to her.
  "It's impossible," I decide. My lists tend to be exhaustive: I hate to leave anything out. I've surrounded myself with books, and I

113

wouldn't give up one of them. I've built up a library in the course of doing freelance editing and proofreading and indexing—the kitchen skills of publishing, I call them. Some of the books I've worked on have become part of my working library—the *American Heritage Dictionary* and the *Illustrated Handbook of American Birds,* for example. I always think it's nice when a publisher gives me a copy of a book I've worked on.

My daughter stops wasting her time on me and goes off to make her own list. I am divorced, a single parent writing and editing in the middle of unironed laundry and unfinished casseroles. I look around my desk—actually, it is not a desk but the dining table; my children must eat in the kitchen—and suddenly I realize that I do have about half a dozen books that are in constant use when I am engaged in writing. I would have said that I could never make a list of less than a hundred, but now I can see that there is a kind of natural geographical selection. There are just about six titles in reach of my right or left hand that can be consulted without my rising or shifting my position too much, except when I have to reach the very last volume of the dictionary, which simply requires sort of lying back along the shelf that runs at a right angle to my work table, the way a piano player might lie along the keyboard to reach the farthermost key.

If I were making that list, I'd have to put *Webster's New Dictionary of Synonyms* first because it's the closest to hand. This sort of thesaurus is a very useful book to a writer, perhaps more useful than a dictionary, because often when I look up a word, I'm not looking for a definition. I'm looking for another word, one I can't quite get. If I can't make that jump to the word I want, I use a book of synonyms.

A. Alvarez once wrote an essay on Sylvia Plath in which he accused her of keeping a thesaurus beside her typewriter and of not washing her hair. I expect that Mr. Alvarez has forgotten that it was one of the worst winters in memory in Britain; the pipes were frozen and everybody was on strike. Plath's *au pair* girl had just left her with the total care of two infants; possibly any hot water went to washing bottles and nappies. If he has forgotten that, then I hope that Mr. Alvarez may find the foxy smell of Sylvia's hair one of those indelible memories that come in a rush on one's last breath.

The next book—the next in point of proximity—is my dictionary. I have several (a writer never relies on just one—different dictionaries have different strengths), but I am going to put the *Oxford English Dictionary* on my list and count it as one title, although I have the thirteen-volume set. Not the reduced-type, two-volume set that you have to read with a magnifying glass, but the full set with entry words in eighteen-point bold and the text in generous twelve-point Century. I got it in the course of a romantic liaison with a man I worked for, and never, never for one moment have I regretted it. It is the most wonderful dictionary in the world. Of course, it is organized along historical lines, with the earliest use first. (The first definition of *liaison* is "a thickening for sauces; also, the process of thickening.") Often you must read several columns before coming across the particular sense of the word you are searching for. But look what you have seen in the meantime! The infancy of a word, its change with historical or social conditions, an example in the memoirs kept by Lady Anne Fanshawe until the year 1680, or its use in 1779 in a report to the rector by Mr. Dougal Graham, skellat bellman of Glasgow. (In contrast, the examples in a recent American dictionary come from Karl Marx and William Burroughs.)

You are probably interested in the details of how I came to own the *Oxford English Dictionary*. I see nothing wrong in a reader's wondering about a writer's private life. It happened like this:

I was working in New York City, in the lower echelons of publishing, trying to support myself and three children and write a novel on the subway as I rode back and forth to the office. A wealthy oil magnate bought the company I worked for, and I was introduced to him. He thought that I might help him write a novel in which he would be the hero. He would come out of nowhere, unaligned with any political party, and would run for President and win. Many beautiful women of all ages and nationalities would be in love with him. I was to do the writing while he "talked ideas." He offered me a modest salary and several hints that we might travel around the world in his private jet looking for interesting locales for our novel. All this was not entirely unbelievable because I also heard him speak of buying *The New York Times* and I was present when someone offered him the dealership for Mack Trucks in the entire Middle East. Most impressive to me, he lent me his charge card for Scribner's Book Store. I suppose I was overly awed by his wealth—I kept telling myself, he must be smart, or how come he's so rich? I worked hard on the book, writing new scenes, cutting the ones he objected to. I mentioned to his wife the importance of travel to a writer, of seeing the places one would write about, of the shock of the immediate, of soaking up the atmosphere of the souk, recording the colors of the sky as the sun set behind the pyramids, and she said to me, "Oh, I think one can do as well by simply looking at the posters in a travel agency."

"May I keep the *OED*?" I asked the oil magnate when we mutually abandoned the novel after eighteen months and one hundred dull pages. I had learned by then, if he had not, that this is not one of the ways in which fiction is written.

Another book I keep handy is the *Encyclopedia of Symptoms*. It contains more than 650 symptoms covering the entire existing range of human diseases and disorders. If you are a writer, you are probably aware of how often one of your characters comes down with something. At least my characters do. I have to know which symptoms signal a mysterious, baffling disease and which will allow a dramatic recovery. I need ailments that will serve as an excuse for getting out of sex and ailments that are fatal. Right now, I am working on a story in which a character must die because, for reasons of plot, I need to have his wife married to somebody else for a change.

I nearly always have a character, whether I'm writing a novel or a short story, who likes to quote. You've known people like that, haven't you? I don't have a good memory myself for passages from literature. When I was in college, I had a good short-term memory, and I could tell you who said almost any line from Shakespeare, but in general when I am working, I have to rely on collections of quotations to supply my characters with something to say, and the one I have on my desk now is *The Quotable Woman*, edited by Elaine Partnow and published in paperback in two volumes by Pinnacle Books. I like it because the quotes have not been overly used. (Yes, this is one more area where women have been discriminated against. They have been underquoted.)

Next to this, the smallest book on my desk is a metric conversion book. I use it mostly for nonfiction, where matters must be accurate. In fact, I use it mostly to calculate whether the thing I am writing about is larger or smaller than a football field, because editors always say that readers want to know.

The last book on my list of books that I can reach without getting up from my work table is a *Thesaurus of Epigrams*. It's nice to throw in an epigram once in a while. It leavens. The Greeks were the first to make up epigrams. The Romans did it even better. Martial, working on his epigrams, invented the punch line. He would do anything with his last line—cynical, obscene—to get a reaction. The Romans wrote their epigrams on stone or wood or metal. Today, epigrams are written on T-shirts. Another daughter is just back from a trip to Houston. She is wearing a Houston T-shirt that says,

"When the Going Gets Tough, the Tough Go Shopping." Wouldn't Martial have liked that?

I have just come back to my work table. I had an idea, but it didn't work out. I thought that if I could touch a corner of my chair with one hand, and then stretch myself across the floor, I could just manage to touch with my toe the *McGraw-Hill Encyclopedia of World Art,* which is on the shelf on the other side of the couch. The point is, then I could include this work on my list, and it's one of those reference books that always gives you more than you're looking for. For example, once I looked up Benedetto Croce, because he is always being mentioned as a top twentieth-century aesthetician, and I wanted to see what he had to say about balance and tension in art. When I looked him up, I read that when Benedetto was a child in Italy, the earth opened up and swallowed his parents. And this child became a philosopher! Would you? Would I? Wouldn't you just say, Well, the universe is both impersonal and deadly? It isn't every reference book that can confound you like that with chaos and order.

Six reference works. I've managed to limit myself for once. Although if a South Florida hurricane struck—or Benedetto's earthquake—I might quickly revise my list.

Typecast
by Michael Lawrence Williamson

Mike Williamson was, for a while, the editor of a Midwestern city magazine. He quit to run a games arcade, and maybe the same affinity for the mechanical that prompted that job switch prompted him to write this brief confession—a tale, you might say, of acquired dyslexia.

Open the lid of my head and find ribbons and pulleys and platens inside. Allow me to smile at you and you'll see two rows of keys that say "QWERTY" and "ASDFGH" sprouting from my gums. It must be true. I'm becoming a typewriter.

Or at least I'm starting to think like a typewriter. Which isn't supposed to think at all. So where does that put me?

It puts me in a situation where, when hand-writing a note, I will print *samll* instead of *small*. That sort of transposition is something I do all the time at the typewriter. It's an error in coordination, a simple matter of a finger on my left hand hitting its appointed key a moment before the finger on my right hand does its job. It is not a mental error. It shouldn't be a mental error. So why do I print *samll* when I work with a pencil? No error in coordination is possible; a single hand is putting down all the letters.

Yet I do print *samll*. I am becoming a typewriter.

I would be less sure of my horrific transformation if my only error were the occasional swapping of letter positions. But I find my hand, like the hands of the cursed in horror movies, doing things I have asked it not to do. Worse yet, my hand does things that I never specifically prohibited it to do, because I never dreamed such errors were possible. (I am increasingly tempted to call such errors "glitches," but glitches afflict word processors and I am not a word processor. Yet. I am a typewriter.) Witness my habit at the keyboard of allowing my ring finger of my left hand to drift, as if pulled by a pocket of excess gravity stationed below the *x* key, so that I often type the *x* when I mean to type *s*. Nothing to worry about. Error in coordination. I never could hit a baseball worth a damn; how can you expect me to hit the *s* key dead center every time?

So why have I caught myself printing words like *xmall* when hand-writing something? No pocket of excess gravity lurks under my notebook, pulling my ring finger down to scribble *x* when I mean *s*. That misbehaving finger doesn't even touch the pencil. I am right-handed. Is it some mental mix-up caused by the fact that *x* and *s* sound alike—the same sort of mix-up that sticks "a pocketful" in your head when you're trying to think of "apocryphal"?

No. It is not. It is because I am a typewriter.

At the keyboard, my uncoordinated pinkies tend to linger on the shift key, so that the second letter of my word is also capitalized. APril showers bring MAy flowers, and all that. Keyboard error. Pure and simple.

Not so simple. Not when I catch my hand printing *APril*, unbidden, into my notebook.

What's next? Will I start printing nonsense words if I grasp the pencil at the wrong place, the way my typewriter pounds out nonsense if I start touch-typing when my hands aren't on the home keys? Will I lazily print the letter O when I really mean to print the number *0*?

Or will I ignore the problem?

Yes. I'll ignore it. That's what I'll do. But it won't be easy. This is no samll problem. (Oh no!) This is no xmall problem. (Oh LOrd!)

What's a poor typewriter to do?

LaffStar
by Alex Heard

*Of course, we don't believe that Alex Heard needs the help
of techno-giggle software to write his humor. Maybe because he was likely selling it before such software was even
available. But since he's willing to credit LaffStar for his
success—some of it, anyway—I'll point out that LaffStar's
work has appeared in* The New Yorker, Harper's, Esquire,
The New Republic, *and . . . "oh yeah,* Vanity Fair," *Alex
adds.*

Each week I get ten to fifteen letters that go something like,
"Sir—got any advice for the fledgling humor crafter? And could
you take a glance at the thirty or forty items I've enclosed and if it's
not too much trouble submit them under your name to an editor
who's used your stuff and if the guy takes any you could say I did
them instead and I'd give you a percentage? Thnx."

Having myself often been eyeball-to-envelope with the cutting
geometry of the SASE, I take these queries seriously and answer
each one. I skip the normal chestnuts ("Read your Perelman, your
Wodehouse, don't write drunk. . . .") and get right to the fact that
many writers today simply don't want to face: The new information technologies have already hit the laugh-production biz *hard,*
and to make it in today's humor market, tomorrow's humorist must
get techno-savvy—*today, now,* tomorrow may be too late—and
though that term could mean something else six months down the
road, right now, today, it means scraping up the cash to finance a
micro with enough RAM (64K minimum) to drive the *indispensable* LaffStar humor-processing software package, $395.95 from
Mirthro. Forget everything else.

Expensive, sure, but nobody said writing didn't require sacri-
fice, and can you really afford *not* to own a system that in addition
to all standard word-processing functions offers:

Idea Nixie: LaffStar is programmed to crash (the top-of-the-
line SuperLaffStar for "voice" computers will simply groan) if you
start to keyboard any one of the thousands of ideas that its memory
recognizes as bad (parodies of local news teams, updates of "Jab-
berwocky," etc).

120

Phony Phunny Name Generation: A real time-saver. Have you ever spent hours searching for that "just right" gag name for some ridiculous character? I know I have. With LaffStar, I simply type in the character traits I want ("SEXY, but DUMB"), hit control/FUNNY NAME/execute, and within seconds I've got seventy-five beauts like these:

Whuddabody Concubina

Va Va VaVoom

Poozy Giggles

Scantilly Attired

Canna Sayneaux

Baud Interface

Idea Production, Verification: Using telephone modems to access huge info data bases like The Source and the Dow Jones news/ retrieval system, LaffStar can, *while I sleep,* sift through mountains of cultural input—news, sports, movie reviews, encyclopedia entries, recipes, stock listings—generating great gag ideas that I then key into the program's WRITE, FUNNY mode. LaffStar can also tell me if an idea has been done, when, in what language, and if it's "safe" (a computer term) to do it again.

Just to give an idea of the program's fecundity: in a single six-hour period, LaffStar produced 134 tart, laff-filled ideas, including these babies:

1. "The Gospel According to Mort." Hilarious. A lost book from the New Testament is found, and it's outrageous. Mort is a sassy wise-guy Jerusalem nightclub owner who sees things they didn't tell us about in Sunday school. His bar features a shifting menagerie of crazies, including most of the disciples, Judean streetwalkers, and a comic named Hahakkook who tells jokes that were already dusty back then:

"I was in Beersheba (*applause*). Who let the seals in? Anyway, this beggar asks me for 5,000 shekels for a glass of wine. I go, 'Wine is only three shekels!' He goes, 'I know, I wanna drink it in Moab!' "

2. "Isaac Stern and Isaac Hayes . . . Together?!!??!" Sounds great, but only the title has come through so far.

3. The *definitive* spoof of the gifted-child craze. This one's set in a

special philosophy-for-children elementary school called Casey Existential. The place is full of world-weary second graders. It starts:

> Waiting. Waiting. Waiting. It rains, but they will not let us in
> before 8:45. Marcie chalks a doleful poem on the four-square
> court:

We are the Hollow Kids,
Our allegiance is pledged,
But the flag hangs limply,
Our lives are six empty time blocks,
Vised in a void,
And our lunch totes are skimpy.

4. A no-mercy parody of the poetry in publications produced by
state affiliates of the National Education Association and American
Federation of Teachers (one problem with LaffStar—it can't weed
out ideas that aren't likely to have broad appeal. Still, the execution
is first-rate):

With SAT scores still declining;
Parents, politicians, children whining,
For higher standards we are pining.
As we see these thorny missions,
We can mope and gripe and fuss,
Or we can start with the admission,
That the enemy is us.

No, LaffStar is not perfect. Besides producing too many poetry ideas, another major glitch is that it—we—can't always finish
the stories it starts. The most vexing of these, "The Only Way You'll
Ever Get My IBM Selectric II Is by Wrenching It from My Cold,
Dead Fists," is a hilarious caper that has literally been driving us
batty for months. LaffStar has gotten me in a fix it can't seem to get
me out of.

The piece plays on the comic reluctance of journalists and
writers to replace their rusty old typewriters with word processors.
(Much of LaffStar's work deals with this.) Taking the concept to its
nutty, illogical extreme, LaffStar has *me* be just as dead set against
giving up my hi-tech (but now outdated) Selectric II. Crazier, my
"last stand" is set in an impossible Southern town full of computer-
literate cornpones who—well, wait, here's how it starts:

> Last summer, like millions of Americans, I retreated to the
> countryside to work on the Great American Novel (run FUN-

NY TITLE, NOVEL search). Because other famous writers are from there (search better reason), I went to Mississippi.

When I got there, to my cabin, I saw this taciturn, grizzled old cracker working inside it. I said to him

(control/DIALOGUE: SOUTHERN AMERICAN/execute):

"¡Hola! Soy de los Estados Unidos."
"Si, hay muchos edificios en la ciudad."

(control/DIALOGUE: AMERICAN, SOUTHERN/execute):

"Hello, what is your name?"
"Them whut know me calls me Jimminy Ricketts."
"What are you doing to the cabin I rented for the summer?"
"Yawll the novelist? Howdy. Ahm installing a dedicated power line. That will pre-vent power surges fum making yawll's word-prahsayuser crash."
"I just need a plug-in. I use an electric typewriter."
"You mean . . . yawll don't word-prahsayus?" He removed his grimy hat and scratched his head. "How you move tay-uxt? Dee-fine and dee-lete?"
"Scissors."
"Well I'll be durned. Well sumbitch."

And on. Anyway, word travels quickly (" . . . with the speed of a 55-cps line printer" is how LaffStar put it) that there's this city feller who don't word-process. Soon there's a steady procession of little rednecks and sheriff's deputies coming out to the cabin for a look.

Eventually the town's mood turns ugly—one night as I'm changing my lift-off tape, a Computerland ad circular, wrapped around a rock, crashes through my window. The next morning my lawn contains the charred remains of an old Underwood #5. . . .

Then the climax: After making a valiant front-porch speech before a robed and hooded gang bearing torches and a Compaq (topic: the right to process information as one chooses), I, the typewriter, and the romantic interest (a Miss Rose-of-Sharon B. Gizzard) flee through the canebreak and swamp, emerging two days later at a Shell station on I-55.

I need change for my emergency phone call—I ask the attendant, who toothlessly grins and opens the *computerized cash register!* He laughs maniacally, truckloads of angry rednecks pull onto the lot . . . *Noooooooo!!!*

You get the idea. Now you tell me, how am I supposed to get out of that? LaffStar's answers are no good (a sample: "I scream long and loud, then . . . I wake up . . . Mom is saying it's time for school. . . .").

Anyway, I've given up, and LaffStar has crashed the last four times I put it on this. When the next generation of enhanced humor-processing software hits the market in years to come, maybe, but meanwhile, I still need an ending.

Maybe what this lacks is the human element. The computer, after all, is only a tool, it's only as good as you are . . . *as you are.* . . . Say, all you people who write me, I'll bet you could come up with something, eh? Tell you what: I'll pay 5 percent upon publication, for all endings used.

My New Old Typewriter
by John Brady

John Brady was my predecessor at Writer's Digest. *One day I walked into his office to find his Selectric II gone, replaced by a stately cathedral-style manual typewriter. I appreciated that typewriter, because at home I had one of similar vintage, though of different brand. I appreciated it all the more when he explained to me, and to* WD *readers in the article that follows, why that typewriter had appeared in his office.*

I'm doubly proud to include "My New Old Typewriter" in this collection. It's a well-written article in and of itself, but it also represents the spirit of WD's *Chronicle section, from which most of the articles you're reading in this book were taken. John Brady, you see, concocted and instituted* WD's *Chronicle page.*

When my father died, he left few relics for a son to remember him by: a baseball inscribed by the 1948 Yankees, given to me that year with the understanding that I would be a Yankee fan forever; a few letters that he wrote to my mother in 1951, promising to cut back on his drinking and hoping for a reconciliation; and a little plastic Model T Ford that he made for me when he was in the hospital dying. That was April of 1952, and I was nine years old. My father was thirty-three.

The baseball has not aged very gracefully, I'm afraid; and my allegiance to the Yankees, like the autographs of Joe DiMaggio and teammates, has faded some with the years. But the Model T remains essentially true. The car is blue, including the driver, but my father—a meticulous man with an eye for detail—used red, white, and black paints to give the car some realistic flourishes. Thus, the fenders are black, the seat cushions are red, and the little blue man behind the wheel is wearing a white suit. As a youngster I played with the car and managed to lose a right front wheel and a left rear fender. Lately, though, the car has been parked on desks where I have worked in the world of editing and writing. I have spent scores of hours in old toy shops around the country trying to find a matching Model-T kit to restore the car to my father's careful standards—

without luck. Even now the little blue man, glued for life to his seat behind the wheel, stares at me as I poke at this paragraph. Collectively, I have probably spent more time looking at the little blue man than I was ever able to spend looking at my father.

My mother remembers my father with a lump in her throat to this day. When she met Frank Brady in 1940, he was timekeeper for a company that was building a reservoir in the Catskills for New York City. Each night he would bring his beautifully handwritten records back to his room and sit at a table dominated by a gray Underwood manual. Then, using forefingers and a thumb, he typed his meticulous charts for the payroll office, filling the columns with numbers and percentages and dollar signs along a well-traveled top row.

I have some photos from those early years—pictures of Frank and Leona at Jones Beach, laughing; pictures of the three of us at a picnic somewhere in New Jersey, and around a Christmas tree in an apartment in Yonkers, New York. I have some later photos of my mother and me on my grandparents' farm a hundred miles from the Yonkers apartment where my father stayed when the marriage fell apart. We were at the farm when word came that he was dead. My parents had been separated for four years, and I didn't comprehend what was going on. Understanding came later as the facts drifted in, and, like most people who lose a parent early, I began a spare-time search for my father in the few things he left behind. There wasn't much.

During my college years, I used holiday vacations to visit the old neighborhood in Yonkers, to talk with my father's only surviving aunt, and to browse awhile in the bars where he used to drink beer and bet on the Yankees. I went to the old apartment building once, and a tenant actually remembered Frank and Leona from back in the forties, and yes, they had a little boy. But while a few people had some memories of a marriage that had vanished, no one ever went into a closet or drawer to take out a pen, a fishing pole, a pocket watch, a *thing*—saying, "Here, this was your father's." No, what the breakup hadn't shattered, the early death destroyed. Dad, I learned, had difficulty keeping a job after the separation; he sold the apartment furnishings to meet one scrambling need or another. Whatever was left went to charity when he died.

And so it was with a sidelong glance at serendipity that I found myself at a Postal Service auction, bidding on a gray Underwood Deluxe Standard that I took home for $10.01 and the privilege of restoring. Let me tell you that it is easier to get parts for a forties-ish

Underwood than it is for a plastic Model-T *circa* 1952. I found a repairman named George who grew up on Underwoods in the forties and knew how to make things work again, and I found a company in Chicago with a boneyard of old Underwood parts, and for less than $50 my Underwood was back in working order. Some of the keys were obliterated (yes, along the top row), but a white crayon, borrowed from my daughter's schoolbag, filled the indentations brightly—and today my old typewriter with new life has replaced the big electric self-erase beauty that used to hum in my office. I find the experience of sitting down to my new typewriter genuinely exhilarating, and I think the little blue man in the Model T is pleased, too.

If you are a writer, you know the phenomenon that occurs when you are racing with your thoughts at a keyboard, trying to keep up, keep up, get ahead of them—then all of a sudden the machine is controlling you, taking you, as it were, by your hands on a journey down the avenues of memory and, if you are lucky, into new arenas of discovery and understanding of the past.

I sit here some mornings looking at the white sheets that go through my typewriter, wondering if this Underwood isn't the very machine that my father used for timesheets—and now it is a time machine of my own.

No, as James Joyce observed, you can't bring back time; it's like holding water in your hand. But as a writer you can—and perhaps must—drink deeply from the past, if only to know the shorelines of tomorrow.

section six

"AND THEN HE BECAME AN EDITOR"

Tales from Both Sides of the Editor's Desk

I am both editor and writer. I don't know which side of the desk I like best, except the side I'm standing on at a given moment.

This dual role hasn't resulted in any sort of split personality—not that anyone has told me about, anyway. Instead, it has shown me that editors and writers aren't the natural enemies many people—including too many editors and writers—imagine them to be. They are partners. Business partners. Partners in an odd business.

These partners serve the reader, the person paying cash for the words the writer is writing and the editor is editing.

But my dual role has also shown me how snags and personalities and miscommunication can prevent such teamwork from reaching its ideal goals.

This section, then, also has a dual role: to examine both positives and negatives of the editor-writer relationship, and to allow editors and writers to understand each other a little better in the process.

Part One
From the Writer's Side

A Perfect Day for Broccoli Spears
by Pat Zettner

When I wrote to Pat Zettner—a college instructor whose work has appeared in YM, American Home, Seventeen, *and* Cricket—*and asked her permission to reprint this piece, I toyed with the idea of asking her if I could* adapt *it. I was fairly certain that she would appreciate the joke.*

But I didn't ask her that, maybe because I consider the problem discussed here to be as serious as Pat does. We write to describe the world, to help the reader and the writer alike to understand it. We don't—we can't—tiptoe around the keyboard and write with the goal of presenting some idealized universe, one that an arbitrary set of school marms (of both sexes, and whether they're teachers or not) somehow dictate should exist. We can't try to construct a fantasy world, one in which there is no violence, no feel-

ing, no ice cream, *and hope our readers will believe it's
true. At best, that's an odd propaganda. At worst, that's
the stuff of which accusations of "Big Brother" are made.*
*I won't go as far as to begin ranting and invoking Big
Brother. But I won't joke about the subject, either.*

When I sold "A Perfect Day for Ice Cream" to *Seventeen,* I
thought it was a fun short story about a teenager coaching her little
sister's soccer team. I never guessed that it was prime textbook material. Still less did I suspect what lay ahead in the wonderful world
of basal reader adaptation.

Nearly two years after the *Seventeen* sale, I returned from a
convention to fish a bulky Scott, Foresman envelope from my mailbox. I ripped open the flap, devoured the first paragraph, and
danced my middle-age spread down the middle of the street in pursuit of my convention friends' departing car.

Waving the letter in my friends' faces, I babbled my delight.
One of my stories was to appear in a textbook. Resurrected from
charity book sales and dusty library stacks, it would live again! We
rejoiced together.

My friends went home, but the euphoria lingered. I floated on
air for hours before I cast an inquiring eye on the key word, *adapt.*
There were, I realized, some photocopies included with the offer.
They would tell me precisely what had been done with my story.

Seldom, surely, has elation died so quickly. I recognized my
name on the credits, the names of my characters, and the barebone
elements of my plot. But somewhere the narrator's humorous, personal style—for me, the heart of the story—had vanished.

From that same somewhere, big words had invaded the narrative. Well, not big words, exactly. Words like *utter* and *encounter.*
Perfectly good words in their place, but not ones I use every morning before my breakfast coffee. The sort of words my narrator
might have used in a term paper but never, never in a friendly chat.

"Vocabulary exercises," I muttered. My hard-won colloquial
style had been sacrificed on the altar of vocabulary drill.

I agonized. It was the first time anyone, ever, had offered to reprint my work. The first time anyone had offered me pay for no
work at all.

My teenage daughter admonished me. Since this particular
story is loosely based on her experiences, it is special to her. "Don't
do it, Mom," she said. "Don't let them print it like that. They
bought it because it was fun to read, and then they took out the fun

parts. No one will enjoy reading it."

She was right. My pride and my principles said so. But my greed said that freelancers are pitifully underpaid, so I'd better take the money and run.

In the end, principle prevailed. I held out for a better adaptation. "Maybe you people at Scott, Foresman would say, *I encountered my buddy down on the corner, and he uttered a few statements,*" I wrote, "but nobody I know talks like that, and I don't intend that my characters will either."

Whoever said that virtue is its own reward never had turned down a reprint check. I couldn't have felt worse if I'd set fire to every dollar individually. Not that the publisher was offering me all that much money. But my first reprint. . . .

Some weeks later, Michael McGhee, a Scott, Foresman editor, phoned. My regret had been wasted. His house still wanted to use my story. And after comparing their version with the original, he could see my points. All of them. I could try my hand at adapting if I chose. But, he suggested, it might be better if he did the rewrite. After all, he had spent ten years as a textbook editor and was familiar with the taboos.

I agreed to an in-house rewrite. But I found the paranoia about taboos amusing. I'd taught in college. I was a pro writer with a reasonable degree of common sense. I'd have known what to avoid. Sex and sexism, of course. Violence, racism, and profanity. Drugs and alcohol. Religion, most likely, unless you wanted to be caught in a crossfire between creationists and Madalyn Murray O'Hair. A hefty list once you started counting, but I could have handled it. How many other taboos could there be?

I had a lot to learn.

In time, back came Adaptation II. This time I was lucky. McGhee had treated my story with skill and with all the respect a writer could hope for. He even explained his omissions.

I began to see what he meant about taboos. My narrator, Carol, could not call her little sister "pest," even though the story as a whole clearly showed their affection. *Implied disrespect to siblings,* read the notation. When her parents failed to bail her out of an awkward situation, she could not say wryly, "So much for parental guidance." *Implied disrespect to parents.* She could not describe her little sister's superb goal-keeping as "playing kamikaze ball." *Possible ethnic slur.* I didn't quibble. My original story was much too long for Scott, Foresman's purpose. Something had to go, and the deletions weren't critical.

But the rationale behind them troubled me. In the house where I live and love—hang on, you're in for a shock—we get annoyed with one another. All of us, adults and teenagers alike, have been known to show annoyance, irritation, and yes, disrespect. Sometimes we shout things that make *pest* seem like a Leo Buscaglia hug. I began to wonder what it would be like in a textbook world where a kid couldn't even imply disrespect.

And what was this noise about ethnic slurs? The reference was *complimentary,* for cripes' sake.

I was glad I didn't make my living as a textbook editor.

By the time I agreed to Scott, Foresman's adaptation, I thought I had learned my way around the never-never land of textbook taboos. Presently, along came Houghton Mifflin, wanting to use the very same story for a similar high-interest, low-reading-level text. Fresh surprises were in store.

Their version was competent, smooth reading, close to the original. All the way to the final page, that is. That's where the story is resolving itself. Against all odds, Carol's inept team of rejects has just won a soccer game. She has learned that the opposing coach, Ron Jameson, did not cheat against her as she has reluctantly believed. And most miraculous of all, he seems willing to forgive her hasty misjudgment of him.

Standing in the chill drizzle that has dampened their game, Ron asks if her team is going to celebrate its victory.

> I shivered. "We're all going to the ice cream parlor."
> "Makes sense," he agreed. "A perfect day for ice cream. But just in case you'd like something warmer, I'll be waiting at your house when you get back. Pizza sound hot enough? Or chili burgers?"
> My mouth dropped open.
> "All in the line of duty," Ron said, straightfaced. "Got to set my boys a good example. It's rotten sportsmanship to let your opponent freeze."

That's how the *Seventeen* version had read. Now the specifics of ice cream and pizza and chili burgers were gone. Ron was talking vaguely of "a second celebration" and of not letting your opponent celebrate alone. Carol, who had once inspected her bedraggled appearance in a mirror behind the soda fountain, was now peering into the depths of a mud puddle. A mud puddle? What was going on?

That wasn't the whole of it. My story was no longer titled "A Perfect Day for Ice Cream" but simply "A Perfect Day." A necessary change, it turned out, since those two corrupting words, *ice cream*, could not be printed in any HM text.

I had learned to live with the omissions of *pest* and *kamikaze*. I could have understood omitting *pot* and *speed*, even *light beer*. But *ice cream*?

It seems I had run afoul of Houghton Mifflin's junk food list. The publisher had proscribed a lengthy list of foods after an entire series of textbooks was rejected in California—a series attacked by a health-food lobby because of a single birthday illustration featuring cake and ice cream. Sorry, said my editor. The ban was not negotiable.

At home we waxed helpful. Why follow the nutrition slant only halfway, we wondered. My son had an idea for retitling. "How about 'A Perfect Day for Broccoli Spears'?"

"Or carrot sticks," suggested a friend. "Better yet, bean sprouts. Can't you just see the victory celebration at the health-food store?"

My daughter had the last word. "I think," she said grimly, "they should call it 'A Perfect Day for Censorship.' "

I fumed. I fantasized anonymous tips to the American Dairy Association. I dragged my heels granting permission. Finally, the editor called me, requesting a commitment.

"I don't like the ice cream bit," I complained.

"No more than I do," she said. "It's scary." It was still not negotiable.

She explained the Houghton Mifflin viewpoint. They tried to produce high-quality textbooks. But if the textbooks weren't adopted by the schools, the quality never reached any students. Better to compromise where necessary and produce the best salable textbooks.

Possibly a rationalization. But publishers, after all, are not publicly funded service organizations. I couldn't quite convince myself that they should be knights in armor, protecting us singlehandedly from the demands of special-interest lobbies. That's a job for informed citizens, who must involve themselves in textbook selection processes, demanding quality and common sense.

So, buying into Houghton Mifflin's pragmatism, I agreed to their revisions. And my story, cleansed of ice cream, chili burgers, pizza, and other possible perversion, appeared in *Orbits*.

Don't be misled by my story. I'd love to go on selling to textbooks. It means income and exposure. And I've adopted a rationalization of my own. My stories seem livelier and more relevant to teens than many of the stories my kids have yawned their way through in school. And, corny as it may sound, I care about textbooks. I'd like to give the great captive audience condemned to read them something they'll *enjoy.*

I've got another story that does just that, too. Kids like it. The magazine editor said so. "The readers identified strongly," she wrote. So I've been looking it over lately, giving it the Textbook Taboo Test.

By the grace of God or the spin of fate's wheel, I never once mentioned ice cream. Didn't mention parents or siblings, so I'm in the clear there. Oops, I had the kids eating pizza again. Circle it in red to be scratched. And I named one character Sylvia Fineberg. A perfectly nice character, so far as I can tell. Still, those ethnic slurs are tricky little devils, always slithering out unawares. Better switch to Jane Jones.

Uh-oh. When Cathy, the main character, loses the lead role, she questions the teacher's integrity. I can see it now. *Probable disrespect to teacher.* Maybe even *definite disrespect.* I can't let pass a case of definite disrespect, but I'm dealing here with the heart of the story. What to do?

Maybe Cathy could be cheerful about Mrs. Zinzemeyer's decision. But then I have no plot. Maybe someone could select the cast by secret ballot. But there goes credibility. Nobody does that in real life.

Of course, nobody studies her reflection in a mud puddle, either.

And on the Fourth Day, He Rested

by Joe Mooney

*I once wrote a comic novel in which—for the purposes of
an easy one-liner—I concocted a fictitious* Reader's Digest
Condensed Bible.

The novel remains unpublished. The then-fictitious
Reader's Digest Condensed Bible *does not.*

*Which is, I suppose, all to the good. Because if my book
had seen print, it would have been subject to Joe Mooney's
incisive criticism.* Cutting criticism, *I suppose you might
call it. Criticism as cutting as this "review" of the* Reader's
Digest Condensed Bible, *which originally appeared in his
column for the* Seattle Post-Intelligencer.

It is impossible to predict at this point what effect a condensed
version of the Bible will have on the publishing industry, but theo-
logically speaking, my guess is that its impact will be enormous.

With the announcement by the editors at *Reader's Digest* that
they had successfully penciled out 40 percent of the verbiage and di-
vinely inspired throat-clearing from sacred scripture, the theologi-
cal principle may have been established that salvation, like professional football, is a game of inches.

I was saddened, of course, by wire service reports that Biztha
the eunuch was gone altogether from the new *Reader's Digest* Bible.
I confess I'd never heard of Biztha to that point, but it seems to me
the process of making him a eunuch had already subjected this unfortunate soul to as much editing as any man needs.

Not so, decreed the editors of *Reader's Digest*. Along with
what remained of Biztha, their deletions included seven out of every
ten words in Exodus, Chronicles, and Deuteronomy; a good deal of
St. Paul's rhetoric ("Paul got a little carried away," editor Jack
Walsh explained); 10 percent of Jesus's words, plus a number of the
psalms. The Twenty-third Psalm, for example, is now the Thir-
teenth because some of those preceding it have disappeared. Obviously, the meticulous numbering of chapters and verses that

marked earlier, windier versions of the Bible are now meaningless.

To genuinely understand editing and the pain it causes, a person has to be a writer (or a eunuch). As H. G. Wells put it, "No passion in the world is equal to the passion to alter someone else's manuscript." The first editor I ever worked for couldn't spell, he knew nothing about grammar, and his writing made laundry lists and tabulations of soup ingredients seem thrilling by comparison. The only thing he knew about the English language was that he didn't like the word *that* and he spent many satisfying hours—satisfying to him, at least—torturing the language to avoid using the word. I worked only two months under him and *that* was fifteen years ago, but to this day I take enormous pleasure, and consider it exquisite revenge, using *that* whenever possible. (Yes, I know the Lord said vengeance was His, but I'm counting on *Reader's Digest* to edit *that* passage out.)

I can recall an instance in which I phrased something very carefully to avoid using a horrendous sports cliché, only to have an editor blot out my words and use the cliché instead. I've even had correct factual material altered by editors to make it wrong. Occupational hazards.

At times like the above, it helps to know others have suffered at the hands of editors, too. William Shakespeare, who had nearly as many hit plays as Neil Simon, was extensively rewritten by Dr. Thomas Bowdler in 1818, to remove the passages Bowdler found offensive. "I want a book I can read to my son," Bowdler said, announcing publication of his *Family Shakespeare*.

When Margaret Mitchell sold movie rights to *Gone With the Wind*, she did so resigned to the certain knowledge that her work would be mangled by Hollywood. "I just hope," she said, "that when they're done with it, the North still wins."

And now that God Himself has been rewritten by *Reader's Digest*, I seriously doubt the rest of us will get much sympathy.

I haven't seen the new, abbreviated Bible, but having read a number of issues of *Reader's Digest* as a child, I expect the style will read like the Gospel according to Tonto. I always suspected the Lone Ranger's sidekick of being a closet *Reader's Digest* editor. His dialogue—"Me-get-horse."—was the essence of brevity and it conspicuously lacked "the three R's" that *Reader's Digest* considers anathema: repetition, rhetoric, and redundancy.

If by some chance the new, shorter version of the Bible catches on, I may offer one myself that will be briefer yet. With modern earth-moving equipment, for example, there's no reason why Creation should take six days (I'd cut it to three). For some time I've felt that six commandments (on one stone tablet) are all anybody really needs—and more than anybody really follows. And in my Bible, there would only be six original tribes of Israel (if more proved necessary, NFL Commissioner Pete Rozelle could oversee an orderly expansion). Finally, wherever possible, I'd schedule more doubleheaders: David vs. Goliath and the Battle of Jericho on the same bill. That sort of thing.

Otherwise, I have only one gripe about the original version of the Bible: I can't stand Charlton Heston. Had I been the author of Exodus, I assure you Moses would have looked like Alec Guinness.

Part Two

From the Editor's Side

Barn's Brown Belly
by Mary Folger

This is all I want to say about this piece (other than thank you, Mary, for writing it):
Prepare to revise your opinion about editors.

The voice on the phone is shaky and elderly. "Are you the editor?" it asks.

I admit with reservations that I am. I have reservations because I am a sucker for shaky and elderly.

"Well, I have a story for you," the voice says, "and you better get out here and pick it up right now, because I'm ninety-four, and I don't have time to be foolin' around."

In my world, such requests are not exactly unexpected. Freelance material, no matter how unorthodox the presentation, is always welcome. Freelance writers are my link with sanity, semi-solvency, and reality. The freelance submissions that cross my desk are sometimes even usable—and my magazine needs anything usable.

I should explain.

The magazine I call mine isn't really. I'm just one of several idiots who decided ten years ago to put out a regional publication. Our baby would be small, we decided, but it would be of high quality. It would be beautiful to behold, report the nice things happening right around home, highlight area history, and do its best to preserve local heritage.

It could even make money, we thought. It would be simple.

We certainly were.

The outcome of our carefully laid plans was not a magazine. It was an octopus on roller skates.

Today our octopus and its drivers have received their share of awards—but they have not been financial. Our command post is located in a basement crammed with furnishings rejected by more self-respecting basements. Issues are put together on things made by my father, and on an out-of-tune piano, a three-legged buffet, and a clothes-line running from the water heater to the furnace. The *pièce de résistance* is the toilet in the darkroom.

Our dreams of a profit-making venture have fallen by the wayside. Our goal now is to break even. As a result, freelancers are always paid too little and usually too late.

Put it all together, and the moral of the story is that we often get the kind of manuscripts that we can afford. We're fortunate in that frequently we get a lot more. A dozen or so regular writers provide us with neatly typed, double-spaced submissions with a minimal number of sentence fragments, dangling participles, and split infinitives.

Another two or three times a month, we receive submissions that are informative and/or entertaining as well as accurate, and that include an author's name and complete address, a telephone number, and, if the moon is right, a self-addressed, stamped envelope.

This is not, however, what I expect.

What do I expect?

Nothing boring, at least not from my aspiring freelancers.

They send me things like articles about barn's brown belly. It took a lot of reading to figure out that a barn's brown belly is, in laymen's and editors' terms, a hayloft.

I expect the immortal works of my novice writers to be loaded with alliterations. "Preserving the Past" has been submitted dozens of times, and "Pictures of the Past" isn't far behind. "The Soothing Semetery South of Suburbia" came in only once. That was enough.

I also expect my writers to be so intrigued by the words they are using that they sometimes forget the people to whom they are speaking. One writer especially liked "media-slicked world of suburban sybarites and nocturnal nymphs." I wasn't sure my media-slicked readers would.

Creativity does not stop with words. My freelancers are creative in all kinds of ways. That's why I expect manuscripts to arrive in Spencerian script on flowered stationery, to be put together in book form and bound with masking tape, to be trimmed to within a quarter-inch of the copy on all four sides, and to be typed totally flush left with extra spaces between single-spaced paragraphs. (I did not expect, but received anyway, one manuscript, hand-lettered à la the writer's latest calligraphy course.)

I expect to receive proof positive that a high percentage of my would-be writers are teetotalers who do not, under any circumstances, imbibe in dictionaries, and that they also think Roget is perfume, that Bartlett is a financial institution, and that Strunk is something that once smelled bad.

As a result of my magazine's dedication to local heritage, I expect my writers to put protagonists who should be wearing moccasins in French heels, and to find that if the footsore protagonist is indeed wearing moccasins that he is wearing them spelled wrong. This also occurs when the writer attacks area Indians. My area Indians lived in long houses; my writers prefer putting them in tee-pees, tippis, or TP's.

It doesn't bother me too much—I've learned to expect it—but receiving an article about Jonation Smith raises the hackles of our research editor. She becomes hysterical if the next reference to Jonation has him Johnathan, and, before the article stumbles to a conclusion, he has also been identified as Johnothan, Jonothon, and Jonathan. Some of those old buggers did have names with unusual spellings, but not too many of them had five.

Also among my expectations is at least one challenge per issue along the lines of "ge Ubduab wabdered qyuetkt tgriygg tge dbse ybdergriwtg ub. . . ." This is a problem when we can't break the code, and the writer, who hasn't kept a carbon or copy of the manuscript, can't imagine why we can't translate and can't remember what she said anyway.

In my search for usable material, I rather expect to find the lead on page 14 and the conclusion on page 3. If I'm exceptionally lucky, I find a well-developed middle in the middle. If I'm not so lucky, I expect to find that there is no lead, that most of the article is conclusion, and that what middle I can find hops, skips, and jumps from page 1 to 5 to 9 to 17.

I also expect to receive some submissions from writers who have never read my magazine. I know this involves jumping to conclusions—they don't tell me they've never read my magazine. I just sort of assume it when they send material about natural areas in the Rocky Mountains to a regional magazine south of the Great Lakes.

What other memory-provoking submissions do I expect to find in my manuscripts-to-do cardboard box? I expect to find too many written seemingly for the purpose of curing my insomnia, and some do the job quite well. I expect almost as many to include the work *unique* seventeen times. I expect the stories that can be told in 250 words to be written in 2,500 and vice versa, and nice little five-letter words to be replaced with synonyms of twenty-five.

I don't really expect my novice freelancers to register objections to rejections, but it happens. Many of the objections simply question my editorial judgment, professionalism, and ancestry, but one came from a real positive thinker. It began: "I wish to apply for the position of the editor who is rejecting my work. . . ."

I suppose, somewhere in the real world, where buffets and pianos are kept in their place and where freelancers are properly compensated on acceptance, that editors don't expect—or accept—my kind of submissions. It may even be that, at some point in the future, that day will come for me.

But, in the meantime, I'm not sorry that I've been introduced to a barn's brown belly. I wouldn't have missed the soothing semetery for anything. And that ninety-four-year-old who insisted that his story be picked up was a heckuva nice guy.

I'm not too sure sometimes about this magazine business. I think I might be able to flush my baby octopus, complete with roller skates, down the darkroom without too many regrets.

But my freelancers?

I'd miss them—my freelancers, my friends.

And Then He Became an Editor

by Paul Hemphill

*Paul Hemphill's résumé notes simply, "Always a writer."
That's pretty much true. He has written for* TV Guide, Atlantic Monthly, Sports Illustrated, Reader's Digest, Life,
and other major publications. His books include The Good
Old Boys, Long Gone, Too Old to Cry, The Sixkiller
Chronicles, *and* Me and the Boy, *and he's at work on an
epic novel about the Cherokees and the Trail of Tears.*

*But there was a brief span that makes the claim "Always
a writer" only pretty much true. This is the story of that
short lapse.*

This is how it happened. Hemphill had been a sportswriter
and sports editor in more towns than he cared to talk about—Atlanta, Birmingham, Augusta, Tampa, Tallahassee—and then
worked his way into the daily "general column" business in Atlanta
and then San Francisco. Along the way he wrote five books and at
some point got out his calculator and figured he had published
about seven million words. *The New York Times* and *Newsweek*
and a lot of others loved him and he took to lecturing at various
places around the country. He appeared thrice on the *Today Show*
and once on the *MacNeil-Lehrer Report* and once a week he was
heard by seven million people on National Public Radio's *All
Things Considered.* He was also heard by his ex-wife's lawyer. They
wanted the $13,000 arrearage. So Hemphill, the famous author,
had to take a job.

Jim Dickey, the poet, had already warned him about such
madness. "It's going to ruin you and rob you of your senses when
you sell out to the bastards at the bank," Dickey said. Hemphill's
lawyer put it more properly when he said, "The time has come for
you to do not what you *want* to do but what you *have* to do." And
Hemphill's old man, a seventy-year-old truck driver from Alabama,
slammed the message home: "You got a *real* job yet, boy, or are you
still trying to *write* for a living?" So Hemphill—rippled by all of this

advice and admonition and general breast-beating—took the easy way out. He took an honest job.

That, in itself, wasn't easy. First he began calling all over his town, Atlanta, asking favors. He had been a big columnist for five years or so and he had friends around the city. So he began soliciting people to write affidavits saying he was "generally unemployable." Three editors complied. These letters were to be sent to Hemphill's ex-wife's lawyer. Hemphill felt good about the whole deal until, on a Friday, he called an old friend who ran *Atlanta* magazine.

"Jack, do me a favor."

"How's that?" said Jack Lange.

"Just sign a letter saying you won't hire me."

"You available?"

"What's this?" Hemphill said.

"I need somebody as senior editor bad."

Oh, Lord.

"Try to make it at 9 o'clock Monday morning."

So that is how Paul Hemphill became senior editor of *Atlanta* magazine.

Hemphill, like most writers, had regarded editors as the Holy Ghost. Writers seldom, if ever, meet them in person. They generally perceive them as The Enemy—people who sit on the twenty-eighth floor overlooking Fifth Avenue in New York and reluctantly tear open our manuscripts, then spill coffee on them, then stash them in a huge pile of others, then go out for a three-martini lunch, then return and can't remember your name or your article—and about all we know about them is what we hear from other writers. *Sid, now, Sid goes to lunch about 1 o'clock. But you can usually catch him in a good mood around 3.* Or, *Gerry turned me down on Wednesday but he had a good weekend on Long Island with his kids and he bought the piece on Monday.* Editors. Who *are* these people who control our lives?

It didn't take long for Hemphill to find out. He had been on the other side of the typewriter for most of his life and now he had a chance to find out how the other half lives.

The salary was $18,000 per year. It was a fifteen-mile drive just to get to work (Hemphill had to buy a ten-year-old car which ultimately cost $2,000 once the transmission and the brakes and the starter and the tires were taken care of), but the perks were decent. There was a free phone and free parking and good insurance.

But then there was the other side. What you had was a writer who had spent his adult life at home, alone, with a typewriter. A person who had read and written at his own leisure. And spent whole days pondering things and playing with his babies and walking around the neighborhood and speaking with his neighbors and doing some more reading and then going to the typewriter by himself to do more typing. You throw somebody like that into the corporate world of research surveys and the like—he in his jeans and his T-shirt and his tennis shoes and his baseball cap—and you got trouble.

A writer, suddenly becoming an editor, runs into a hellhole of problems he never knew existed. The basic writer—working off instinct, simply born with the talent, never having to go to Yale or whatever to *learn* how to write (you can't *learn* how to write)—is confounded by rookies who throw up questions such as the following: When do you write? How do you write? What do you write? How do you do a query letter? Should I send an SASE?

The answer, my friend, is that there *is* no answer. The Great Hemphill, Answerer of All Writing Questions, had no answers because there *are* none. What you do is try to make a buck to stay alive—write for *Mademoiselle* if you have to—but keep on writing. The best advice you probably ever received, anyway, was probably from your first-grade teacher. "Write about what you know."

Teaching is overblown. Teaching and editing are in the same ballpark. The best editors Hemphill has ever known are like patient mothers. They keep a long tether on you and let you wander into the night and expect you to come home at a decent hour. They let you go and explore and then come back with a report on what went on today Out There. You can't teach or edit. You simply kick them out and see what happens. If they are street-smart they will come home with wondrous stories.

Hemphill was generally proud of his year as a magazine editor. He introduced fiction and poetry to *Atlanta* magazine and he drew some new writers out of the closet and he upgraded the quality of writing. But his proudest moment probably came in the name of Jingle Davis. Jingle lived on a Georgia island and was a mother twice by the age of twenty-two. All she had known was the island and her husband and her boys. Now she was about forty and divorced. So she constructed a platform tent atop her Volkswagen and headed west, by herself, and did eleven thousand miles and wrote about it.

"Collect call for you," the operator would say.

"Who from?"

"Jingle Davis."

"Where's she at now?"

"Phoenix."

"Put her on."

And Hemphill and Jingle Davis would talk for an hour. The car was holding up. She was heading for San Diego. Then she would go to Seattle. She had run into a biker and they had spent a night together in the woods. She was "finding myself," as hoped, and she had a "hell of a story if I make it back." And she did, indeed, have a hell of a story.

"Just call me whenever you get lonely," Hemphill said.

"Maybe I'll never be lonesome again."

"That's what it's all about."

"Bye."

"Bye."

When Hemphill rang off he lit a cigarette and threw his boots on the desk of his cubicle and listened to the intercom signaling ad salesmen to *their* cubicles and figured that was enough. He desperately wanted to be Out There with the Jingle Davises of the world. He wanted the free-spirited life of the writer, which he had always lived, and he'd had quite enough of the secure life afforded by a salaried/sanitary/free-parking and insurance/benefits job. First he wrote a letter of resignation. Second he called his lawyer and his insurance man and his tax man and his wife. Then he wrote a check for $125 toward the first month's rent in his new "office," the former barbershop of an old hotel in downtown Atlanta, where he moved his typewriter and picnic table-desk and some Union Mission furniture. And, finally, he moved back to the only side of the typewriter that really counts.

section seven

"HERE TODAY, GONE TODAY"

Tales of Appearing in Print

You remember the crucial instants in your life, those that rattle your heart or deflate your heart or energize your heart.

I remember where I was when I heard John F. Kennedy had been shot (at home from school, fourth grade).

I remember my wife's precise phrasing when I proposed ("William! You're drunk." I wasn't.).

I remember the evening John Lennon was shot (it disgusts me even now that I had to learn it from Howard Cosell on Monday Night Football).

I more than remember seeing my first words in print. I feel that sight. The memory is tucked into my brain just behind my eyes so I can see it better than I

*can see these words as they go down onto the type-
writer paper.*

The words weren't even mine.

*I was in high school, and was a manager (i.e.,
towel-distributor, time-keeper, and equipment-storer)
for our track team. When we won an important meet,
I phoned the sports department of the* Milwaukee
Journal, *some miles north, with my carefully written
brief story on the victory.*

*The next day, there it was. Not my words. My in-
formation. That was good enough.*

*I mounted the story, the whole column inch of it,
on a sheet of aqua construction paper.*

*Why on aqua? Heaven knows. Probably the only
thing I had around. But I can still feel the construction paper as I held the clip, and I can still feel the
words. . . . I don't remember them precisely, but I can
feel them.*

*Here are the tales of others who also feel them,
who remember, or are about to remember, or aren't
sure if they remember at all.*

Literary Limbo
by Kathleen Rockwell Lawrence

*How lucky Kathleen Rockwell Lawrence is. Not only is
this the third time "Literary Limbo" has been published
(as of this writing), but also it's the third time Kathleen has
had to wait for it to see print.*

*The novel she discusses here finally did see print, shortly
after this piece first appeared. The novel was* Maud Gone,
*and though she no longer has the honor of waiting for it
to be published, she can now comfortably enjoy the waiting for other novels, other fine pieces of writing she can
take pride in.*

My first novel was accepted more than a year ago. By a good
publisher, I was astounded to hear. Two months went by between
the acceptance and the signing of the contract. I was worried for
those two months because, despite my agent's reassurances, I was
certain that my editor had second thoughts. I had been found out.
She knew I was a fraud and wasn't literary enough for them after
all. I knew she had told my agent and my agent was working up the
strength to break it to me.

Then, on line for a reading, I met a young lady whose first novel is also forthcoming. We congratulated each other and smiled a
lot. We spoke up so that others on line might hear. Then she said she
wanted it to be published before her thirtieth birthday, and had
asked her publisher to move up the date for that reason. And we had
been having such a nice conversation, too. I couldn't think of much
to say after that, though I did keep smiling. I didn't hear much of the
reading either, what with Time's winged chariot clattering away behind me.

Though I am a new writer, I am not a particularly young writer. I had a wasted youth—fun, but basically wanton. So now I
couldn't wait. When would my editor call? When would we start?
When would we get the show on the road and the book on the shelf?

"Why the delay?" asked my friend, a corporate lawyer. "If your
book were a brief, my firm could have it published in a week."

I told her it's different with a novel. I don't know much about
it, but I told her there's editing and proofreading and something
called galleys.

My friend shrugged. "Like I said . . . a week." This didn't help me much.

Then I got the contract and, more important, the check, half of my advance. I knew the editors were going to publish me after all.

Next, my editor called me and explained that she wouldn't be getting to me for a while. There were books ahead of mine on her list, and they had to be taken in sequence. And before the book would be published, there would be discussions, rewrites, artwork, galleys. Everything takes time.

I suddenly didn't care. A delay in the rewrites might mean a delay of pub date. (You see I'm learning the lingo, too.) I am terrified of whatever pub date holds. I like it here in limbo. Limbo is OK with me. I'll take it. Because even though I don't get to sing Hosannas, I haven't been banished from the kingdom.

Not yet, O Lord, not yet.

Now I think that it is precisely because I am not in my first youth (thanks for the euphemism, H. James) that I can savor this time all the more sweetly. I see quite clearly that it may be my shining hour. Who would wish it gone?

I've worked for sixteen years as a teacher, and, while I've been fortunate in that position, and very fortunate in my colleagues, life had, let's say, its predictable side. No great pleasures, no real terrors. (I work in a good school.) Which is why I started teaching school in the first place. You see here one facet of my neurosis.

The rest of my psyche will be laid bare when my novel is published. It's autobiographical in the way of many first novels. Publication means exposure, and that could get chilly.

There are people who may leave me when the book comes out. People I've known from infancy; people who have loved me in their fashion. My novel isn't outrageous, but it is honest, and I have never been honest with these people. I could not be and still have them.

The real me is in my book. The adult. The writer. They are proud of me now. They've never known a writer before. But I fear that they will leave. Who needs them, then? Who cares? I do. The real me. The child. The writer.

My story will be on the street. Everyone will know my shame. Everyone will know my name. Or worse, maybe they won't. Maybe only my family will buy it and see how I've embarrassed them, and for what?

Right now my parents are still proud of me. My child still gets invited to birthday parties by children of nice families. She hasn't been expelled from her school or rejected by her teacher. I haven't gotten us evicted as undesirables from our low-rent apartment. The old ladies on the elevator still smile and greet me.

My husband hasn't gotten fired because he is the spouse of a deviant. In fact, he actually tells his clients about me, a practice that alarms me greatly. I beg him not to, but he does. He's our sole support now that I've taken a leave of absence to Write. Doesn't he know how important his job will be when my principal decides that I'm not a fit example to my students? He says no, that I'll be supporting him soon. He says he believes in me. Which is why I married him in the first place.

My daughter likes my life as a writer because I am around more. I can pick her up myself from kindergarten and take her to Baskin-Robbins. I don't grouch as much when I clean her hamster's cage. We don't have to leave as early: she gets to watch cartoons these mornings. "I'll have to go back to work soon," I tell her. "This time off is just for a little while. I have to go back and make some money."

"Your book will make you money," she replies. "And, it will make you famous." I swear I never told her about famous except to say that it was what Michael Jackson was. I told her this once when she asked about limousines. I told her that rich and famous people rode in limousines. Michael Jackson rode in limousines. Is this what she expects of her mother?

My old friends still like me. They tell me they want to be invited to my publication party. I tell them they might have to throw my publication party. A friend's dermatologist says he'll buy my book, so there's that sale, at least. Someone else says she'll take my picture for the book flap—she has a new Polaroid. Another offers me his family for my next book. (We writers don't work that way, I tell him gently.) My cousin from California took me out to dinner when he was in town.

Also, there's a way of telling who your friends are. People I thought were my friends have inquired after the sales of my book. Don't they know it's not on sale yet, that it's not even a book yet? And if they thought it was at the bookstores, why didn't they go out to purchase it and find that it wasn't on sale yet? Huh, I say to myself, and I think I am right in saying it . . . I don't think the people who said that have any intention of ever reading my book.

But I have new friends to replace the ones who weren't really. I have literary friends, other new writers who send me post cards of Walt Whitman and Virginia Woolf. They call me up and we go out to lunch and gossip literately. I go to readings now. I even gave a reading. A lovely old club has given me privileges for a year. I've been invited to a few literary parties.

I had been invited to these parties before, but it was different. Before, my whole approach was "I'm nobody, who are you?" What I found out was, nobody likes to be nobody, too. In all honesty, I didn't love hanging out with the other nobodies who would have me. People would ask me what I published. I would tell them of my short story in a literary magazine. They, even the other nobodies, would move on. One fellow put it this way before moving on: "Would it take less than a half hour to read your entire published works aloud?" I like it. It was stern, but a little different, and definitely up-front.

Literary parties were kind of tough on me because I'm naturally gregarious and have always enjoyed regular parties. I always brought this expectation of having fun along with me.

Ah, but now I am having fun! You don't just go to a literary party to make a report, but there is that element. If you report well, there is a reward. You get to stand there and casually chat with witty folks, with writers, with the people you have always wanted to be. I can't say I don't like it, because I love it.

My reporting has been going well. I make modest mention of my novel. People say, oh, and congratulations, what a fine publisher, and, what is your name again? I tell them, again. I have told some of them my name each time I've seen them at a party in the past, but I'm glad to tell them again now. I like saying my name. I think that this time they may remember it. At least until the review comes out. . . .

It's like a modified E. F. Hutton ad. Someone nearby says, excuse me, I just heard. . . . And I graciously repeat my name and accept congratulations. It occurs to me that one could work these parties for a year or so without having gone to the trouble of writing a novel.

I don't know how long I'll be able to play these parties like this. I think, in a few months, if my novel is still not out, I'll change my approach a bit, talk about my current project. So far, though, no one's eyes have glazed over.

I have seen this syndrome, the glazing over of eyes. It is horrifying. It is brought directly on at the mention, by a writer, of his work, published only a year ago, unsung and unread.

They ask me when my novel will be published. I say soon, but I'm not sure when.

My rewrites are done now. My editor calls to say they're fine, and that the copy editor has my manuscript. Things are really moving. "Great," I tell her.

Title Misdeeds
by David Jones

As an interlude between freelancing and working as a magazine editor, Dave Jones managed a bookstore. During that time, he would return occasionally to his hometown Cincinnati and we'd get together over drinks. We'd laugh over his stories about people in general and bookstore customers in particular, and when we stopped laughing, I said, "Our readers would like to hear those stories."

"No, they wouldn't," he said, but he wrote this little gem anyway. Dave still believes readers don't want to hear these stories, even though Reader's Digest *reprinted a portion of this a while back.*

David, you're just plain wrong.

Never confuse your reader with facts. Or with fictions. And *never* with the titles of either.

Take it from one who knows. For three years, I managed a large bookstore in Texas. I learned that the customer may always be right in the traditional business sense, but the customer is always wrong when it comes to book titles. Name your book *Surrender at Midnight,* and I guarantee that your reader will ask the bookstore clerk for *Attack at Dawn.*

Most customers are not like that, of course—but I have come to know a special breed of bookbuyer affectionately known as a "mallite," because of his natural habitat: the shopping mall. A typical conversation between mallite and clerk runs something (actually exactly) like this:

"May I help you?" says the clerk as he smiles.

"I want this new book, but I don't know the title or the arthur." (Yes, "arthur." This means writer.)

"Do you know what it's about?" the clerk asks.

"No." (The customer at this point always becomes monosyllabic.)

"Is it fiction or nonfiction?"

"Oh, it's fiction." Then the customer hastily adds, "Because it's true." To show you he does know what he's talking about, he says, "It's this big," a gesture, "and I know the cover's green." For some reason, the cover is always green.

"I'm afraid I can't help you without a title or an author."

"But it was in the newspaper," or "on the *Today* show" or "on *Donahue*." Take your pick.

Your reader delights in playing word-association football. A college student once asked me for *1982*, by George Orwell. Having some fun, I replied: "That book's been updated. It's now *1984*." She said: "I'll take that one then. It's got to be better."

In other fractured fairy tales, Thomas Hardy's *Mayor of Casterbridge* became the *Mayor of Killen*, after a town in Texas. The cartoon cat "Garfield" became "Garfark." Several mallites were convinced William Saroyan wrote *Sophie's Choice*. One customer asked me for "that cookbook by Fanny Hill." I could have shocked her with *that* recipe.

One hapless mother wandered into my store with that blank, bewildered stare I have come to love. "Johnny needs a book for school," she said. "I can't remember the name of it, but it reminds me of a dinosaur."

She didn't understand why I didn't leap to the book. Having had no brontosauruses or pterodactyls in stock for some time, I wandered about the store for twenty minutes while she pleaded with me: "Oh, it's just like a dinosaur. Why can't you help me?"

At last, the relief of understanding hit me. You guessed it. She wanted a thesaurus. Lesson: Don't use foreign terms; your reader is a *tabula rasa*.

Never deliberately confuse your book buyers. They have enough difficulties already. When John Irving's *The World According to Garp* first hit the stands in paperback, it was released with six different covers. Woe unto the mallites. It was nigh on impossible to convince them that each book with the different cover was the same as the other. I considered telling them that everything was the same except chapter ten and, if they wanted the full story, they'd have to buy every edition. When the film came out, *Garp* was given yet another cover and we were all in trouble again.

Your reader has other peculiarities. When your book is published in hardcover, 80 percent of the buyers want it in paperback. When that edition is released, they will then want it in hardcover.

The customer is fascinated with the edges of display tables. No matter how long a book has been in stock, it will sell within the day if it is moved to the corner edge of a table. The next time you're in a shop, unobtrusively move your books to that table edge and count your royalties.

Hope that your masterpiece does not win a major literary prize. John Kennedy Toole's *A Confederacy of Dunces* won the Pulitzer Prize for fiction during the same year as the Janet Cooke/ *Washington Post* controversy—Cooke won the Pulitzer for nonfiction and subsequently lost it when she admitted that she had fabricated sources. We decided to heavily promote *Dunces* and we built an attractive display for the book.

A middle-aged couple strolled by the display. The wife did a Buster Keaton double-take and began to moan.

"Look at that, Harry," she said with a sigh. "Look at that." A great gasp of air hit the books. She grew angrier and continued to exhale, "Look at that." At last she dramatically pointed at *Dunces* and said: "That's a lie. How can they sell that? Didn't you hear about it on the news? It's a lie. He made the whole thing up and they took the prize away. I'll never shop here again." She dragged her husband out of the store, never to return.

But don't be discouraged or disillusioned. The message of your Great American Novel will get through to your reader—somehow. Not everyone wants *War and Peace* (or is that *A Separate Peace?*). Our tongue-in-cheek moral is this: If you want to be published, make sure that your book comes in a green cover and that it naturally gravitates to table edges, and you'll see your name on the Bestseller List.

But probably in the wrong category.

Here Today, Gone Today
by Roberta Hershenson

If a tree falls in the forest, goes the pop mind-expanding question, and no one is in the forest to hear it, does it make a sound?

And if that same tree is felled to produce newsprint and no one is around to read what is printed on the newsprint, does the writing on it exist?

Roberta Hershenson, who regularly sells photo-essays, ponders the question.

How do I keep my publication day from ending? the philosopher within me wants to know. *And, if nobody reads what I've written, was it really published?*

The questioning began late one stormy night as I retrieved my evening paper from a snowbank. There, heading the Lifestyles page, I saw a familiar name: mine. Beneath the name, word for word as I had written it, was an article I had mailed to a writer for the paper whose work I admired. As a photographer who was writing for fun, I didn't know where to send short essays and thought this writer could advise me. She had skipped the advice and gone right to the point.

"The editor tried to call you," said the writer next morning when I phoned her. "She loved your article and wanted to use it. When she couldn't reach you, she ran it anyway. Hope you don't mind."

Since the byline was correct and payment was promised, I didn't mind. Not at all. But a chill ran through me as I remembered the snowdrift of the night before. Had the newspaper been buried deeper, I wouldn't have found it. Had it been wetter, I wouldn't have opened it. My publication day would have come and gone, without my ever knowing it.

But did anybody else know it?

I hadn't heard a word from friends, so I called them, ostensibly in search of copies. Their answers were disappointing. "Too busy shoveling yesterday to get the newspaper." "Delivery boy never made it through the storm." "Sorry, threw it out. You had an article in it?"

To add to my disappointment, the newsstands carried no papers from the previous day. There were no copies anywhere, not even one for Mother. I began to feel that my article had never really been there at all. It had vanished, as completely as Cinderella's carriage.

So this was what publication was like: here today, gone today. Nothing in my life as a photographer had prepared me for this ephemeral glory. You can hang photographs on the wall and invite people to view them over a period of time. Pictures have lives of their own, independent of the calendar.

Nevertheless, I continued to write essays and submit them to various newspapers. As more of them were accepted for publication, I began to notice a pattern. Invariably, publication day fell on a major holiday, when lots of people were away. Or the weather was too terrible for people to go get the newspaper, or too gorgeous to sit inside and read it. Or some earthshaking news commanded page one, and everything inside could be hanged. When you come right down to it, there is never an ideal time for an article to come out. One's visibility, finally, depends on people's newspaper-reading habits.

So, I began to judge people by whether they had seen my articles. Those who did received high marks for their thoroughness (going through that whole paper), astuteness (noticing my byline in all that newsprint), and worldliness (proving that here were people who really kept up). Those who didn't fell some notches in my esteem. My first tendency to judge them as journalistic illiterates gave way to a more benign view: nice folks, perhaps, but sadly uninformed.

This was admittedly an egocentric standard, but it helped me cope. If my articles were doomed to disappear with the setting sun, I would value all witnesses to their existence.

After a number of published articles, I eventually came down from my protective high horse. It dawned on me that not everyone who noticed my writing felt compelled to mention it to me. It was even possible that some people didn't like it. Besides, I experienced something new and surprising, something wonderful, in fact. I received notes and letters from people I had never met, telling me they enjoyed my articles and encouraging me to "keep writing." Old friends and acquaintances called, telling me that my writing had touched them. My children's teachers sent messages home, my husband's patients chatted with him about my latest piece. It was intoxicating, relieving. I had readers! Some I knew; most I didn't. But they were out there.

Now I'm not bothered so much when I see stacks of old newspapers piled by the curb for recycling. I don't take it personally if a photo-essay I've worked on for weeks comes out on a glorious Sunday in October, when "everyone" is sure to be out looking at the leaves. I know *someone* will see it. Besides, there are more serious things to worry about. The page could come out blank, for instance.

Now, the philosopher in me has another question. *If you should notice one of my articles, would you save me a copy?*

section eight

"MYTHS AND SHADOWS"
Crucial Moments in a Writer's Survival

In the introduction to this book, I talked about a couple of the working titles we used before deciding on Just Open a Vein. *A working title I didn't mention there was* Rites of Passage, Writes of Passage.

Yes, cute and . . . well . . . obnoxious. But it gives a flavor of the articles in this next section. Here, writers are learning and growing in ways that writers must learn and grow. Some people think that spelling skills and ways of storytelling and marketing strategies are all a writer must learn. Untrue. Each writer must also come to terms with his or her expectations of writing and what writing should be and, ultimately, with his or her own self-image as a writer.

Myths and Shadows
by Bill Spencer

This time, I'm going to let the author do all the talking:
"If I have learned anything since writing 'Myths and
Shadows,' " Bill Spencer wrote to me recently, "I have
learned that I am a human being first and a writer second.
Too much desperation in wrestling a writing career out of
stony circumstances can create joyless, dismal prose. I
spent too many years clutching at the identity and chimeri-
cal career of 'Writer' when I should have been exulting in
the writing.
"I have had to remind myself that publication (a writer's
Grail) is incidental to creation. If the joy goes out of writ-
ing, I might as well stop writing. If I'm not having fun,
I'm doing it wrong."

My college yearbook shows a picture of me crouched over an
old, hunchbacked Remington, a cigarette in my mouth, a seedy,
hungover kid wearing a dirty sweatshirt and old jeans: title this
Writer at Work.

I was nineteen then. I am over forty now. At nineteen I told everyone I was a writer. I did not, however, write. Now I write two
thousand words a day, and I tell most people that I am unemployed.
Perhaps I am overreacting, but I am too familiar with that vast
country of self-indulgence that can be claimed by anyone who calls
himself a writer. I never want to enter that territory again. I might
not write.

That is what I want to write about in this article: the difference
between writing, the profession, and writing, the myth of the great
American free-spirit wild-ass writer.

I began writing because I loved the sound of words, the way
those vowels and consonants could line up, could make statements
of terrible, improbable power. I began writing, I think, for the right
reasons.

In college I wrote a novel about hitchhiking, being true to oneself, and being, coincidentally, a young writer. Halfway through the
book, I shifted to free verse, having discovered that it took a hell of a
lot of prose to fill a single page.

The book was unreadable, of course, intentionally obscure, adolescent, silly. I was, although I was unaware of it, already shifting ground, beginning that transformation from a person who cared deeply about words to a person who posed as a writer and disdained communication, delighting in his own obscurity, elitist and arrogant.

Back then, a lot of people knew I was a great American novelist. They knew because I told them. That is the simplest way to do it. Now people knew why I drank in the morning, rarely attended classes, wore the same sweatshirt and blue jeans for record periods of time, and, unbidden, quoted lyric poets.

One day I told some people in a bar that I was going to Munich. Thus committed, I went to Munich where I drank heavily and cast a keen writer's eye on one of Thomas Wolfe's favorite cities. In the winter in Munich, snow falls, winds blow; there is a distinct chill in the air. That is all I can tell you about Munich. I am sure it is an admirable city, filled with museums and art galleries and beautiful buildings that inspire profound reflection. But I missed that stuff. I missed it while striking the alienated artist's pose over a flagon of beer in one of the vast, surreal beer halls of the city.

Hallucinating slightly, I went home.

I got married.

I continued to be a great American novelist. My wife got work.

We moved to St. Petersburg, Florida, and I wrote a novel about a decaying college and a computer Christ. An agent accepted the novel and a number of publishers said kind things about my writing abilities. But they all confessed to some confusion as to just what was going on and why. The novel was a muddled performance and no one bought it.

But I was encouraged. I had potential. There was no doubt that, when I really applied myself, I would write a good novel.

I spent a year writing the first page of a novel. I would get up in the morning with great resolve. My head would hurt and I would be somewhat shaky from the fifteen or twenty beers I had knocked down the day before, but these writer's scars and infirmities weren't about to stop me. I would read yesterday's page and throw it away. I would go to the refrigerator, get a beer, and return to the typewriter where I would begin the great American novel. A lot was at stake, and I might have two or three beers for courage before plunging in. I would write a page and then, pleased with myself, I would drink another beer while studying the bright shimmer of Florida, that mystical fall of light through the live oak leaves.

Occasionally it would occur to me—or, more often, my wife—
that I should cut down on the drinking. But writers drank! Poe,
Fitzgerald, Hemingway—my Lord, American literature floated on
a great, benign sea of alcohol. The artist, sensitive, perceptive, tragic in his isolation, drank to keep the horrors of reality at bay.

I got a divorce and went to Virginia.

I traveled around, saw old friends.

One day, shaky, unable to swallow the morning beer, I arrived
in a hospital in North Carolina where I told a doctor, "I think I'm
losing my mind."

He squinted his eyes, nodded sagely, and said, "Yes, that ap-
pears to be the case." I had hoped for some reassurance. I wasn't really looking for a confirmation of my diagnosis. I spent a week on
IVs. A doctor suggested shock treatments.

Three and a half years ago, I stopped drinking. I didn't do it
through any great resolve or strength of character. I stopped drinking with the help of many concerned people.

For many years I thought that drinking was a way of life, an attitude. Two years ago I spent considerable time talking to an extremely intelligent woman alcoholic who argued that drinking was
an existential stance. Alcoholism, I told her, wasn't philosophy; it
was pathology. I told her once—and she was properly insulted—
that, if she ever did kill herself, her death would be a textbook example of alcoholism's progression. I still believe that. She continued
to drink. She committed suicide, and I am sure that she felt her reasons were valid.

When I stopped drinking, I didn't immediately return to writing. Drinking and writing were interwoven in my mind. I gave my
typewriter a rest and got routine work. Last November I decided to
try again, and I am presently completing a novel.

There are days when I don't want to write. This business isn't
all poetry and fire. In a piece of writing as large as a novel, there is a
certain amount of verbal glue that must be manufactured. This verbal glue consists of exposition, transition, scene-setting, and it is not
all that delightful to write.

I spent many years in bars with other great American novelists
who were unpublished. I suppose we were mutually sustaining. But,
to my knowledge, we didn't write much. We left husbands and
wives; we traveled to California or Colorado seeking inspiration or
revelation. It is easier to leave a spouse than it is to write a novel. So
why do so many people offer broken marriages and trips to the
West Coast as writer's credentials? I suppose it is because they have

been sold the myth of the great American free-spirit wild-ass writer.

I now know that that sort of thing has nothing to do with writing. There is no lifestyle that identifies the artist. There is only writing. Writers are easy to identify; they write. They fill pages with words. They submerge themselves in their internal worlds, and they don't emerge for long periods of time.

So watch out the next time someone you don't know walks over and says, "Hey, you're a writer, aren't you?" If you were recognized by the tweed jacket and the abstracted air and the scotch and soda in your hand and the manuscript under your arm, you may be in trouble.

Rosellini's Apt Apothegm
by Mark Worden

*I remember Mark Worden from his days as an editor on a
magazine I was about to list in* Writer's Market, *which I
was editing at the time. Mark had apparently completed
the* WM *questionnaire, and perhaps he was being mischievous, perhaps just a bit bored with the lengthy form, but
he jotted in "Kilgore Trout" as the name of the magazine's
photography editor.*

*Well, Mr. Trout is busy being a character in Kurt Vonne-
gut novels, so I doubted the veracity of the claim.*

*That goes to demonstrate that Mark doesn't take every-
thing seriously. And this is the tale of how he came to
adopt that attitude.*

Have a little career anxiety? A touch of a chronic undifferenti-
ated case of What-Am-I-Going-to-Do-When-I-Grow-Up Blues?
There are a lot of cures on the market, from electric blanket therapy
(stay in bed and toast) and hot tub soaks to biofeedback and psy-
cho-babble groups.

I use a form of what has been called "autogenic training." I
talk to myself. *I'm a late bloomer,* I keep telling myself. *Every day in
every way, I'm slowly, but surely, blooming.* It's my prayer. Works
better than a TM® mantra.

I started thinking of myself as a late bloomer years ago when I
discovered these precocious little phenoms who had mastered three
languages and differential calculus by the time they were six. More:
At ten, they had composed comprehensive histories of the world,
and by sixteen they had completed epic novels. Not to mention the
sonnet sequences. And the autobiography at twenty-seven.

Pre-video profligate, I was playing pinball machines (and
cheating). I was learning to smoke cigars (painfully) at the Hog
Trough Drive-In, and trying (unsuccessfully) to pick up girls at the
local skating rink.

I still get nauseated in the presence of cigar smoke and roller-
skating music. Pavlov was right.

Meanwhile, the precocious ones became more prolific.

True, I did write on occasion. I recall paraphrasing *The World*

Book Encyclopedia for a writing assignment in the seventh grade. The subject was "Lions." The MO was "last-minute blitz." Such assignments and the acceptable grades I got set my writing pattern for years to come: Write only when assigned, and leave it until the last possible minute. Then find a reference and paraphrase, paraphrase, paraphrase.

Eventually I did experience a burst of creativity. My first poem. I called it "Test Tube Tess"—a sprightly bit of doggerel about artificial insemination and its . . . ramifications. I was a high school senior. And I was still trying to smoke cigars and pick up girls.

In college I dabbled in poetry—the usual pastime of socially inept students suffering from chronic malnutrition brought on by too much beer and not enough protein in the pretzels.

I somehow grew friendly with the editor of a college literary magazine, and he encouraged me to submit some poetry. I did. To my amazement, he said he'd accept two or three poems.

He picked out a piece of trash I'd included to bulk out my works. "I like this one," he said. "And I think I can find room for these two." He held up two other miserable scraps.

I was furious. He *liked* my weakest efforts. "But what about these?" I asked, waving a handful of poems carved from my very flesh.

"No, I want to use these," he insisted.

I insisted back. I told him he could have only what *I* considered to be my very best work. Or he could have nothing. He decided to take nothing.

I showed him.

In the ensuing years, I wrote bits and pieces. I'd been told I had talent. I knew that. But more important, I had the *feeling* I was a writer. After all, I'd read a lot of books, and I grew a beard.

I became adept at *Inner Writing:* the art of writing in my head. Inner writing gives many of the emotional satisfactions of being a writer, without the drudgery, disappointment, and risk of putting words on paper.

It was hard, *hard* to write—especially when I had the excruciating sense that each syllable was set down for eternity. That was the lesson I had learned throughout my schooling: Literary stuff was destined inexorably to be rigorously analyzed by scholars, critics, and graduate students armed with theories, appendices, and footnotes. It was a bloody wonder I could write at all.

The whiz kids were all over the bestseller lists. *I am a late bloomer,* I told myself. Small consolation, but it helped.

The turning point came in Vincennes, Indiana, during the early seventies. The Berrigan brothers were on trial for antiwar capers, and a newspaper columnist proclaimed them traitors.

Traitors, indeed, I snorted. I dug out my old typewriter and two-fingered a mean letter to the editor. I wrote it and rewrote it. I put the jingoistic columnist in his place.

I enclosed a note with my letter. The note carefully explained the importance of publishing my letter "as is." I warned the editor not to take anything out, because I had crafted some searing comments that the People needed—no, deserved—to read. I had set the record straight, and I wanted no one to tamper with my version of the truth.

I waited a couple of days. No letter. I went down to the newspaper office and spoke with the editor. He remembered my letter. He found it in a pile of papers littering his desk. He handed my letter to me and turned to walk away.

"Hey, wait," I said. "Aren't you going to publish this?" I meant to be assertive, but I think it came out like a cross between a whine and a sneer.

The editor curtly replied, "We don't publish anything without reserving the right to edit."

I sighed. This was obviously going to take longer than I thought. This . . . *journalist* was a shade on the thick side. Dense. "Listen," I persisted, "I put a lot of work into that letter. Every word counts. If you cut anything out, it loses its meaning."

"Words," he mused. "Words are just like bricks in here. We use them to build what we need."

Like bricks? I was stunned, stupefied. But only for a moment—my moment of truth. "Wait. Go ahead and use it any way you can." I flashed an ingratiating smile through my beard. Inwardly, I grudgingly conceded: A bit of the truth may be better than none at all.

It was an important lesson. Being a slow learner, a late bloomer, I had taken thirty-four years to learn it. Meanwhile, movie companies were vying for the screen rights to the bestsellers written by my precocious peers. I quit trying to smoke cigars. And I finally picked up a girl.

Then I took another important step. I showed my consort some of my verse. She usually smiled a lot and nodded, but this time she said, "I'm not sure what you mean here."

I quit writing poetry for five years. When I went back later and reviewed my early poetry, I had a hard time understanding it and I realized what an excellent decision I had made.

Insight does not ensure instant success. I started out slowly. A book review in a newsletter. A column in a local newspaper. No money, but experience in writing and publication.

Then I was invited to write a column for a trade paper. I had several publications in professional journals. And finally, an article I got paid for. And a story sold. Small presses published a few of my poems. Wait: I placed a poem in *Rolling Stone*. Freaking far out, if you get my drift—even though they did get my name wrong. *Wark Worden*.

What happened to the precocious ones? They became rich and repetitious. Their work got feeble, flabby.

My work was getting strong, lithe, and versatile. Sure I sometimes lamented that I was taking a long time to hit my stride. When I sniveled, my partner, Gayle Rosellini, would try to encourage me. "Remember, you're doing your apprenticeship," she'd say. "You're doing all right for a late bloomer."

She said that once too often, when I was in the midst of a profound existential malaise. I grouched back, "What the hell's so great about being a late bloomer?"

"Be glad you're a late bloomer," she said with a smile. And then she formulated Rosellini's Apt Apothegm: "The best thing about being a late bloomer is that you never have to worry about becoming a has-been."

The Big Three-Oh
by Tom Shroder

One Sunday morning I opened the Cincinnati Enquirer's
*Sunday magazine and discovered this story, the strongest
piece of writing I had seen in that publication in some
time—and how nice to see that it was about writing.*

*Well, actually, it was about a moment in life, using writ-
ing as a vehicle for the tale. But the same can be said of
most of the chronicles in this book.*

I met with Tom, then a special projects writer for the
Enquirer *and now an editor on the* Miami Herald's *Sunday
magazine, for lunch one day, and we talked about the article, and about writing, and about the big three-oh, which I
had tallied myself not long before. We agreed that this
would touch* Writer's Digest *readers, no matter which side
of thirty they were on, no matter how far off, or how far
past, that landmark age was for them.*

*When we first published this article we pointed out that
in journalistic terms, "thirty" means "the end." But in real-
life terms . . .?*

Not long ago, I idled my car at the exit booth of a downtown
parking lot, trying to extricate my wallet from the pocket of my
jeans. Just as I wrenched it free of the overstuffed seat and tangled
shoulder harness, I was taken by a rush of emotion. My hand
trembled as I fished for a bill, and I drove off slowly, momentarily
uncertain where I intended to go.

This was no emotion I could name: neither entirely unpleasant
nor very comfortable. It was something like butterflies in the stomach, only less giddy, far more serious. I had the sense of something
coming up very fast from my blind side.

Whatever it was, the feeling began to come more often and
with greater urgency—usually, as at the exit booth, in totally inap-
propriate situations.

Several weeks before my birthday, I began to suspect it had
something to do with my turning thirty.

The subject came up one night when we invited some new friends for dinner. The woman was a published novelist, a fine and serious writer. She had, she said, passed her thirtieth birthday, oblivious. She had been too busy working.

After initial success with both fiction and criticism, she went for the heart of what was in her. For seven years she labored to build the manuscript. She worked until she had exhausted something and left it in the pile of bond paper. Only now was she discovering that her book would not sell.

Dinner was nearly over, the dishes still on the table. She had made her proclamation with such natural casualness that it took me a moment to comprehend the weight of her meaning. She stopped a beat, as if surprised herself. I began to think that this was the first time she had ever spoken of discovery.

In somber tones, she spoke of the "Death of Print," and sounded as if she meant her own.

"I put everything I know into that book. I was so caught up in writing it, I slipped right past all those life crises I was supposed to have." She chuckled. It was a dry sound, but had real mirth in it. "When I began to see nobody wanted what I was writing, I had the crises all at once."

Though I argued then that turning thirty was hyped beyond meaning, that the hysteria said to ensue was a product of pop psychology and narcissism, at evening's end I saw too clearly that even if an insistence about the exact number is absurd, the crisis is real enough.

Whether it be at age thirty, thirty-five, or forty, sooner or later we all have to press close against that inner certainty that we are exempt—from pain, from failure, from death—and realize how treacherously false an illusion it is.

To say, as I did that night at dinner, that the numerical turning of my age held no terror for me simply was not true. In fact, for many years, I had been anticipating my thirtieth birthday and investing it with a crucial significance.

Of all the things I have ever aspired to, the one I have wanted most fervently is to write fiction. I had few illusions about how difficult that might be, so I allowed myself what I thought was plenty of time, and at the end of all those late nights in exotic cities amidst the roaring fellowship of my twenties, I forgave myself for not staying home to write.

I always told myself I was willing to wait—to watch and learn and build my discipline—as long as I wrote at least one novel. By the time I was thirty.

It hasn't happened.

That our friend had chosen to speak so plainly about her disappointment moved me to consider my own. For the first time in my life, I seriously considered the possibility that I would never write a novel. Or that if I did, it might be inconsequential. And even if I wrote an important work, it might never be published.

After our guests had gone, the dishes and the evening done, I sat on the edge of my bed on the same spot where I had first touched feet to floor that morning. I looked at the lamps and chairs and closets, all in their accustomed positions, and suddenly wasn't sure that the whole day hadn't been imagined. Morning and night, birth and death, separated by nothing more substantial than steam.

A few weeks later, I met a woman at a professional workshop in Columbia, Missouri. We began talking at dinner, and soon were speaking as if we had known each other for years. Toward the end of the evening, I discovered that she would turn thirty the same week as I would.

I told her about my feeling that it all had some telling significance I couldn't grasp.

She smiled tolerantly. For her, the significance was crudely obvious.

"I was raised to think that whatever else I did, my only real purpose was to have children," she said.

At twenty-nine, she was extremely successful. In fact, she was at the workshop to accept a national award. But to a large extent she still considered herself a failure. She had no children.

Apologizing for "the heavy-handed symbolism," she told me that she was scheduled to spend her thirtieth birthday in the hospital recovering from an operation to remove a diseased uterus.

I told her I was sorry. It made me feel petty for agonizing over a stillborn novel.

She said, "Maybe you won't be a novelist. Maybe you weren't meant to be one. What's wrong with being a good journalist? Sometimes I think the real problem is clinging so desperately to some vision of what we think we should be, when really that's not our fate."

In the miserable days of early spring, the tremulous, uncertain emotion that followed me merged with the bleak weather. I had gone in a snowstorm to an interview on the edge of town. The taxi back downtown was a half hour late, and when it came, I discovered I had no cash. We drove around in the treacherous slush searching for a bank machine so I could pay the rapidly inflating fare.

Though it was late when I finally got back to town, I decided to stop in the office to check my messages. I was really looking for a message that with one burst of information would change everything. Realign all possibilities.

What I found was a page ripped from a desk calendar, folded and stuffed under my phone receiver. It said, "Call your brother."

My brother is not the type to call at work for a chat. Sundays are more his style.

"What's up?" I asked brightly, waiting to feel the force of the blow I knew was coming.

"It's Dad," he said.

My father had coughed up some blood. When he went in for tests, they discovered a cancer growing in his lungs. It was inoperable. Now my brother was telling me on the phone that our father was dying.

That night my stepmother called from home. She could barely say hello before she broke down sobbing.

"Tonight is the night I'll use to pull myself together," she said.

Later, I walked into the darkened room that is our home office. Across the back alley I could see the teenage ballerina practicing in her apartment, her hair up in a towel, the strength of her young dancer's body clear against the flesh-colored leotards. In the cold light of the television, she kicked and pirouetted while the sturdy figure of her mother stooped to the laundry.

I was captivated by her litheness, her buoyancy, and the powerful sexual force of her movements.

The moment was heavy with something unutterably true, yet I tried to utter it. I typed: "We don't know anything. We live in a dream, the reality of things flickering beyond our comprehension until we are consumed by what we refused to see, shaken from our fantasy as if it has counted for nothing."

The weekend of my birthday, I decided I would celebrate by putting up a swing set for my six-year-old daughter.

It was the first weekend of good weather. The air was fragrant and bracing, the light so fresh it felt as if someone had torn the lid off a box we'd all been living in.

I drove out to a suburban mall. The guy on the loading dock came out with the heaviest box in the place, about twenty feet long and only two feet wide, maybe two-hundred pounds. It teetered out the back of the Toyota wagon I had borrowed, threatening to fall out at every pothole. When I got home, I laid the fifty or so unlabeled metal parts out on the lawn with the five bags of hardware and fittings and the large sheet of gibberish instructions. It took me fourteen hours to sweat the ill-fitting parts together.

The last hour, my daughter came out with her friend and camped at the foot of the slide, asking every few minutes, "Can we climb on it? Are you done? Please can't we just go down the slide?" When it was finished, they fell on the swing set with the fierce hunger kids have for fun.

I stood in the kitchen, watching their play, exhausted, but very happy. For the first time in a long while, I felt solid and complete. That night, I fought off exhaustion, took a shower, and walked with my wife, exploring the neighborhood and the big fairy-tale cottages that sprout among the trees on the secluded side streets.

When we got back, we looked over the swing set and saw that the ground was uneven and one side was sinking into the soft dirt. In my fatigue, the realization hit me like a rock in the chest. It would have to be taken apart and moved.

I let my knees buckle and sat on the damp grass, trying to calm down. My muscles were raw with the memory of all the difficult junctures and joints of aluminum tubing, the stripped bolts and scraped knuckles. I watched as the lopsided silhouette of slide and swings grew into a giant, entangling web of failure.

When I finally collapsed into bed and closed my eyes that night, I jolted upright with pain. Something must have dropped into my eyes when I was working and irritated them all day. It felt as though the insides of my eyelids were lined with nettles. I was too tired to keep my eyes open, but it hurt too much to let them shut. I turned thirty at midnight, wondering if I would have to go to the emergency room.

The next day, a good friend called from a city on the other end of the continent. I knew I would have to tell her my bad news. She had some of her own.

Her arthritic hip was giving her pain. When the doctors had inserted the artificial joints four years ago to battle progressive deterioration, they left long crescent scars on her hips that her mother, trying to cheer her as she wept before the mirror, said gave her the look of a Grecian urn. Now those miracle joints had failed. She was on crutches. The pain was bad.

She had to decide if she would have another operation for a new, improved artificial joint. At thirty-three, she was looking at a

lifetime of such operations, and each time the chance of a potential-
ly fatal bone infection went up something like 12 percent.

"What I have to face," she said, "is that I've reached the point
where, as far as my health is concerned, I have nothing better to
look forward to."

But despite the sad news, she told funny, delicately observed
stories about her friends, the town where she lived, and her plans.
Her voice held that same bright magic it always had.

"It's me, Dee," she had greeted me, high and melodic, curved up
at the ends like a peal of laughter.

When the call was over, I hung up in an extraordinary state.

I knew, finally, that it had taken at least thirty years to have,
and appreciate, a friend like that. To hear her voice as I heard it
then.

At once I felt embraced by all the special people who had filled
my life, the things I'd seen, the stories I'd heard. Through it all ran a
fine, rare kind of courage. It was the courage that lifted Dee's voice;
that let a woman gain a vision of fate at the loss of her womb; that
moved a writer to give her life on paper, then chuckle at its rejection.
It was the courage to live, not in the face of loss, but heedless of it. It
flowed from their hearts as naturally and irresistibly as the furious
energy of children at play on a new swing set.

The emotion that had been dogging me for weeks broke like a
storm. It was as if a screen had flown open. What had been indis-
tinct was locked in vivid relief: this was no single emotion, but an
ability, a willingness to let down my fears and feel.

My skin quickened to the touch of air. The world poured in the
windows and rushed through the crack beneath the door. Even the
sadness and terror it contained thrilled me.

I couldn't help it. I couldn't stop it.

Dying Gratitude
by William J. Slattery

Bill Slattery has written for a number of important markets: Esquire, TV Guide, Cosmopolitan, *and others. One day he found himself with an assignment to write for the most important market of all. . . .*

A long time ago I was a press agent. Concealed in Brooks Brothers clothing and carrying an attaché case that cost eighty dollars (big bucks then), I called myself a financial public relations counselor. But really I was a press agent, a con artist hired by businessmen to hype their company stock.

I didn't like being a press agent. I was noble and honest and clean and brave, kind to dogs, forever helping old ladies across streets ("Take your hands off me, you fool! I don't want to cross the street! Help! Police!"), saluting flags, and things like that. I was too good to be a flak so I became a writer. I have never regretted becoming a writer. But recently I came close.

One afternoon I walk into the kitchen to turn on the noon news. I wake up spread-eagled on the floor, face up. It is 3:45. I have been unconscious for almost four hours. I have never fainted before. What the hell, I think, everybody faints once in a while.

My teeth chatter, sweat rolls off me in a torrent, I shake all over uncontrollably. Piffle, I think. A passing flu, a minor megrim, a momentary malaise best forgotten. Old people faint all the time. I'm forty-nine. Have to get used to this sort of thing. I pour myself a huge vodka, cover the typewriter, and tune in a rerun of *M*A*S*H*.

No need to trouble my wife with this niggling medical bagatelle, I assure myself, glugging down a second vodka bigger than the first.

The next morning I awake with chest pains. I get out of bed, take a few steps, and crash to the floor. Oh well, I can go to the john later. Two hours later I try again, fall again, crawl back into bed, and ponder whether to die without disturbing my wife who sleeps soundly beside me, or to be a real sissy and tell her I think I am having a heart attack.

The chattering of my teeth awakens her. I am drenched with sweat. I shake like a man working a jackhammer.

A few minutes later I'm on my back in the emergency room of a local hospital staring up into a battery of lights. Two bottles of clear fluid empty into my veins. Serious-looking people come in and out of the room. They do blood pressure tests and an EKG, take my pulse, take blood samples, and do other tests, and while the technicians labor I try to think up some last words, some really good ones, ones that will let everybody know what a great man they are losing.

Last words are hard to think up. Do I have a deadline? Should I make light of my finality? Should I say something wise? How about funny and wise? Should last words be wiser than funny or funnier than wise? What is the market for last words, I wonder. Should I deliver them deadpan? In dead earnest? Speaking of dead earnest reminds me of Hemingway.

I am being watched.

I turn my head. Standing a few feet away is a little man with a stethoscope around his neck. My incisive writer's mind tells me he is a doctor. He holds papers in his hand. His mouth is slightly open. He looks awed.

He approaches my deathbed. He stares down at me, a rapt look in his eyes. He holds up the papers. "It says here you're a writer," he says.

"Yes," I say weakly because I know dying guys are supposed to say things weakly.

"Published?"

"Yes," I whisper, whispering being very in among the dying today.

"Do you have an agent?"

"Yeah. Down in New York," I croak. The croak doesn't come out too good. I have never croaked before. If there's enough time left I must practice croaking.

"I'm working on this novel," the doctor says shyly. "Will you look at it and if you think it's good enough, will you send it to your agent?"

"Yes," I say nonchalantly and serenely. Or serenely and nonchalantly, I forget which.

He clasps both my hands. His eyes shine. Visions of fame, the Carson show and Donahue dance behind his enraptured eyes. He releases my hands. Bowing with gratitude, he backs out of the room. His whole being glows like a medieval painting of a saint. Published! He is going to be published at last! No man on the planet at this moment is as happy as this soon-to-be author.

Before he gets out of earshot I croak with a bit more assurance,

"How long . . ."
  "Less than a hundred . . ."
  ". . . do I have to live?"
  ". . . pages. Double-spaced."
  "No, no," I cry. "I mean how much longer. . . ."
  "Oh," he says offhandedly. "You're anemic. Probably a small bleeding ulcer. No surgery indicated. Maalox and rest and such and you should be home in a week or so. I'll have the manuscript sent up when I find out which room you're in."

  I shut my eyes and a lovely fantasy swims before my eyes. The doctor approaches my bed.
  "Insurance," I tell him. "I write insurance."
  The little doctor looks dismayed. "But your agent in New York. You said you had. . . ."
  "My agent in New York is Equitable Life."
  "Published. You said you were published."
  "No. You misunderstood. I said 'established.' Equitable Life is established. You wanna buy some insurance, Doc? Cheap?" But I don't live out the dream. I drift off to sleep.
  Later, I decline to read the doctor's manuscript. I say I am too weak. Anemic, you know. Besides, I need all the energy I can get to think of those deathbed words, those undying gems croaked weakly.
  I am home now. I am perfectly healthy, my bout with anemia having passed. I practice croaking five minutes every day and a number of my friends have told me that my croak whispered weakly is one of the best they've ever heard. I have not yet written what it is exactly I will croak, but in the end I'll come up with something.

Editor-on-the-Shoulder
by Barry B. Longyear

Few of the articles you are reading in this anthology started out as assignments. Most were submitted on speculation. I rarely assign material for our Chronicle section because I seek power in the writing, not just a good idea treated capably. I seek fresh insights into the world of writing, delivered in tales that hum and crackle a little bit even after readers put them down, as if they were charged with a force beyond electricity. Editors can detect good ideas treated capably in query letters. Detecting hum and crackle is damned difficult.

But it wasn't hard to spot them in Barry Longyear's idea for a story about his "internal critic," the part of his mind that questioned and analyzed his every story—for that matter, his every word. I made a notable exception; I assigned this Chronicle to him.

I thought I might have made a mistake when his first draft came in. It was handled capably, all right, but it wasn't particularly special. I wrote and told him so.

He came back with the draft you are about to read. When it arrived, I opened the envelope and glanced at the lead, as I usually do with assigned submissions before dropping them into my out-basket so that other editors could review them. But I didn't drop this one in my out-basket. The hum, the crackle, the power of the first two paragraphs held me.

In September of 1980, I sat at my desk and tried to concentrate on the pretty things I had placed there. Three days earlier I had become the first science fiction writer to win the Hugo, Nebula, and John W. Campbell awards in the same year. I had a pile of nice mail from readers, and another pile of nice contracts from editors. I added my passbook to the items on my desk. I was making a very nice living at writing, and this was only my third year at it.

I stared numbly at the loaded rifle in my hands. Ending the pain of my own existence was my priority of the moment. The only thing that was preventing me from carrying out this execution was

an overwhelming sense of confusion. Before I pulled my own plug, there was a question that needed an answer: "I have accomplished everything that I set out to accomplish; why is it all nothing?"

I could remember when a kind note scribbled by an editor on a rejection slip was enough to send me happily skipping around the house. I could remember the wild ecstasy of my first short story sale, the feeling of seeing that contract, that first check. I remembered how I felt when I received my author's copies and first saw my story in print. By that time I had already sold another hundred thousand words of stories to the same publication. And just three days ago I had seven thousand fans raising a thunder of applause as I picked up those awards.

"It just doesn't make any sense," I said to my desk. *But then,* I responded, *what ever did?*

A note. I turned to my word processor. I ought to leave a note. If I am going to leave hair, blood, and brains all over my office wall, I ought to leave a note. My machine was on; I set up a new document number and sat back in my chair. A suicide note is like any other kind of writing: there's a right way and a multitude of wrong ways to do it.

"Now, there's an article you'll never see in *Writer's Digest*." I began laughing, thinking of titles.

"Checking Out: Six Dos and Don'ts." Maybe a monthly column: "The Last Word." Maybe a college course: "Denouement 101."

I picked up my thesaurus to look over its collection of synonyms for *cessation*. I was thoroughly engaged in perusing the selection when I awakened to the fact that I was doing it *again*.

"Can't I even write a suicide note without getting sidetracked?"

I dropped the book on my desk. The sidetrack was my usual hiding place from the little creature I call my editor-on-the-shoulder. I have remodeled houses, landscaped entire states, and fiddled away whole lives to avoid writing. I laughed again, thinking that this time I was safe. "The creature can't touch me this time; I'm on my way out." I returned to the suicide note.

How long I sat staring at that blank screen I cannot tell. It was completely dark outside when I gave up and turned off my machine. During those hours, however, I sat listening to my editor-on-the-shoulder.

A suicide note is such a cliché. Suicide is such a cliché. Can't you come up with anything fresh, imaginative? Why don't you just begin with: "The purpose of this suicide note is. . . ."

The end of my life ought to have some meaning, I thought. Surely I can at least check myself out without going through this nightmare of self-criticism. But before I could get the words on the screen, my editor-on-the-shoulder had already processed, judged, and condemned them.

"Maybe I ought to shoot my word processor."

With that piece of brilliant deduction, I turned off my machine and called it a day. Inside of an hour I was drunk, tearing up my house and terrorizing my wife. Moments later I was passed out somewhere.

Fourteen months later, the local campus of the University of Maine honored me with its Distinguished Achievement Award. There I was, a black fog dressed in robe and mortarboard, listening to the university's president read off the reasons why I was worth honoring. It was more than I deserved, yet it was nothing. Less than nothing. That evening I was again before my word processor, rifle in hand, trying to compose my postscript. This time my editor-on-the-shoulder prevented me from even turning on my machine.

—*Such drama! What a tragic figure! Isn't offing yourself with a .22 popgun a little less than convincing? Boy, won't they be sorry when you're gone, ho, ho, ho*—

Two weeks later, in St. Mary's Rehabilitation Center in Minneapolis, undergoing treatment for alcoholism and addiction to prescription drugs, I began the process of learning about me, my disease, and what I can do about both. Among the many things I had to confront was my editor-on-the-shoulder, which is nothing more nor less than a manifestation of what I think of myself. My addiction to alcohol and drugs had not created this monster. EOTS had been on my shoulder in one form or another ever since I could remember. In fact, one of the excuses I used for drinking was to shut up that little voice. Writing for me had always been a war between me and myself, attempting to gain enough peace and quiet in order to tell a story.

At rehab I was told that I am not a writer. I am a human being; that is what makes me worthwhile. Writing is just something that I do. I was told that I need to get my feelings of approval from inside of myself, rather than from others, or from trying to convince myself that I was more important than others because of my occupation.

That sounded like a pretty neat trick if I could do it. How wonderful it would be not to drop into a two-month depression with each rejection I received. Wouldn't it be terrific not to sit wringing my hands about bad reviews and good reviews that weren't good enough? Wouldn't it be great to just be me, instead of using up energy putting on an act? Wouldn't it be heaven to just write and enjoy it? It sounded very, very good. I could hardly wait to try it out.

When I returned home, the first thing I did was try to get back to writing. I could not do it. As I sat before my machine, I got ugly in the head. Millions of ancient doubts, hates, hurts, and resentments leaped into my mind, crowding out lesser things such as ideas and stories. My editor-on-the-shoulder was sober and alert, and I could no longer risk the anesthetic to shut him up.

It's no trouble for me to go out and play with chemicals again The program I am in tells me that we all know that we each have another drunk in us. What we don't know is if we have another recovery in us. I believed this, and I certainly didn't want to go back to the way I was before going into rehab. But a writer who doesn't write is what?

Of course, I remembered what I had been told in rehab: I'm a human being; writing is just something that I do. It was a difficult mental move to make. I *liked* telling people "I'm a writer." It made me "something." It gave the rubes something to focus on while the real me hid behind the screen.

I would try writing again; again I would go ugly in the head. Finally, it came down to a choice between writing and sobriety. At the time I could not have both. So I quit writing.

What am I, who am I, why am I here, who gives a damn? Without this label of "writer" to prop up my false pride and self-image, I was groping around in the dark. I took up wood carving, got lost in video games, became an expert rifle shot (at targets farther away than arm's length), relearned playing the piano, and remodeled my office. I also became immersed in my recovery program. My fellow recovering drunks and druggies would tell me to have patience and give it time. Whatever is supposed to happen will happen, and it will be right on time.

After a year of this leave-of-absence from writing, my life seemed to have some serenity. The new day was something that I approached with eager anticipation rather than dread (what my program mates call the difference between "Good morning, God," and "Good God, it's morning.") One day I had an idea for a story that I wanted to write. Since I was no longer a "writer," I had no thoughts about what might please readers or editors. I had no intention of selling it. Writing the thing was all the reward I needed.

It was the difference between focusing on outcomes and focusing on the activity at hand; between doing something because of what it might get me and doing something for its own sake; between writing to please others and writing to please myself. It was a glorious experience. When I am smart, this is now how I do all my writing. When I am not so smart, I begin edging into thoughts of fame, fortune, and gathering the approval of others at the expense of approving of myself.

I had been using writing as a means to attract applause. When I would get the applause, I couldn't trust it. That's why I had been sitting in the middle of a pile of awards preparing to blow out my brains. My year away from writing showed me that I could live without the applause, and it allowed me to hear some of this applause coming from within myself.

My editor-on-the-shoulder? He is alive and well, but we have worked out an arrangement. If I am honest with myself, if I am honest with the readers, and if I am willing to take the risk to place myself on those pages and share myself with the readers, editor-on-the-shoulder stays away. On the other hand, if I let myself start thinking about outcomes, or resume thinking of myself as a "writer," or try to appear to readers as something that I am not, my creature climbs back on my shoulder, my head goes ugly, and I am paralyzed.

Although it took me an eternity to understand it, the mechanism is rather simple. The more wrong things I do for myself, the smaller and cruddier I feel about myself; the more right things I do for myself, the better I feel about myself. Understanding what "right things" are took the help of a great number of unselfish persons. Understanding what "myself" is took time, patience, and friends. Friends are those folks who tell you what you need to hear, rather than what you want to hear.

Do you find writing difficult? Do you find it tough to get started? Do you find that you hardly ever complete a project, or if you do you stick it in a closet, afraid of rejection? Are you sharpening pencils, arranging files, doing needless research, rearranging your office, daydreaming, stacking wood, or fighting with your spouse, parent, or child instead of writing? Do you get tangled in never-ending revisions, the infinite search for the proper punctuation mark, proud to identify yourself as a "perfectionist"?

If any of the above applies to you, you have an editor-on-the-shoulder of your very own. Trying to ignore this creature, or trying to beat it into submission with success, only allows it to grow unchecked. Success at writing will not remove your creature. Your creature will take whatever success you have and turn it into nothing. Booze and other drugs will not kill your creature. Your creature will use them to control the remainder of your tomorrows.

The solution is to accept yourself, be yourself, and be kind to yourself: a life-long and quite demanding study.

section nine

"ONE UNFORGETTABLE ACCEPTANCE CHECK"
Tales of Culmination

Then comes payday.

So many ways to talk about payment in the writing world: by the word, by the column inch, by the manuscript page. Royalties. Flat fees. On a work-for-hire basis. "We'll cover expenses."

How nice it would be to be able to back off now and say something noble but ultimately false like "But all those methods of payment are not the payoff that writers seek." We want to be paid for our work. Of course we do. We want to be good at what we do; we want to excel. We want to communicate, make a mark, commit any number of other clichés that describe being important. Sure, we want to do all that, but we want to make a living, too.

Still, still, there are the paychecks with no dollar signs on them. There are the moments, like noisy coins, that clink within us when we leap up with the joy that they have brought us.

These are the moments.

This is the payday.

Gold in Them Thar Hills
by Robbie Branscum

Writing has the alchemist's touch: lead into gold. And it has more: gold into more gold into more gold, a self-perpetuation and a perpetual motion as physically impossible as alchemy, yet at the writer's fingertips as they move across the keys.

Robbie Branscum's tale is one of alchemy, as you'll read here. And hers is one of self-perpetuation, gold into more gold, as evidenced by her eleven books in print now, and her awards, including an Edgar from the Mystery Writers of America.

Deep in the Arkansas hills there still stands a small, one-room schoolhouse. I hear it's been converted to a church, but in my mind, it will always be my school with its sixteen pupils and three orange crates of books.

For the seven years of my education, I read those books over and over, and never ceased to marvel that there was a world outside our hills, and that it was peopled with creatures far stranger than the space monsters of today.

I soon found, emerging from the hills, that I was the strange one. Maybe because there were just one of me and a whole lot of them city buggers.

At the ripe old age of fifteen, and my husband not much older, we headed out of the hills in a wooden-sided Ford, to get us some of that California gold "we'd heered of." It was in the early fifties. Blood ran hot in our veins, and greed filled our hearts. " 'Spect we'll make leastways six, seven dollars a day!" We'd grin at each other now and then.

We came off a mountain into the San Joaquin Valley of California with four flat tires, 115° heat, and Lord above, *The Grapes of Wrath* still lived, and we were it!

Our dream of gold turned into a hut in a labor camp, twelve-hour days of picking cotton, stooping, plucking and filling and dragging that long cotton sack. Salt-sweat dripping from your face and oozing down your back.

I learned to cuss in those cotton fields, and to dream as the sun beat down on my head and bent shoulders. I dreamed of the three orange crates of books back in the cool hills, and relived the stories they told, over and over in my mind. And I knew I wanted not gold, but to write stories, to make people feel good or cry or laugh. But, "Hellfire," I cussed under my breath, "I can't spell!"

Yet, the seed was planted and grew faster than the cotton. Pen and paper became more important than food, and I hardly noticed the long hours or the heavy cotton sack dragging behind me. For I already decided I was a writer. I mean, nobody could prove I wasn't, could they? If I said so, I was, wasn't I? A writer could be a writer without being published, couldn't she? But what about a seventh-grade education? I asked myself. "And jist what in the dagnab tarnation do it matter?" I answered myself.

There were whole rooms, even buildings of books called libraries, and I began to haunt them, reading, reading, and reading! Zane Grey, Christie, gothics, Shakespeare, Dickens, names I couldn't pronounce, let alone understand. But I read them anyway.

Cotton picking ended and grape harvest began, and crawling under the vines heavy with fruit, I fought wasps and dreamed on.

Hog Heaven time came with a steady job for my husband and a rented typewriter. I still couldn't spell or type, but being freed from the cotton patch, I had time to love that typewriter, and to spend hours poking out words with one finger. And hours to read. Then suddenly, one fall day, madness overcame me and I wrote! I wrote poems, Country & Western songs. I wrote long, witty (I thought) letters to my friends. I wrote short stories, westerns, ghost stories, poems (religious ones, and, gasp! pant! sex ones!).

I sent the religious ones to *Playboy,* the sex ones to *Reader's Digest,* and the westerns to a magazine run by nuns.

By nab, I really was a writer and had rejection slips to prove it. Most editors were very nice to me; others took one look and tossed my masterpiece in the garbage can. Mainly because I'd never heard of SASE. In fact, I had to skimp on food just to mail something off.

I joined the Famous Writer's School and was immediately flunked. Because the short story I chose to write for them was about some queer hens we had on our farm in Arkansas. (I think the word now is *gay.*) The school did grudgingly admit that it was the most unusual story they'd received.

Years slipped away. I had a child, my husband slipped off, and still I wrote. I sent one of my stories to an agent, who will remain nameless for the simple reason I can't think of anything else to call him!

He sent my stories back, saying, "Miss Branscum, you'll never, ever write a book. I suggest you write to amuse your friends." Then he implied my friends couldn't read anyway.

I was so angry I sat right down and wrote my first book. A pitiful saga of a poor ignorant Arkansas girl who wanted to be a writer. I told all and sundry that I had written a book. I was a writer. When they asked who my publisher was, I coughed, choked, gasped, and asked them how their Aunt Mert's collards were growing.

Times grew desperate—there was no work for me in the small farm town where I lived. My child was growing up, my husband was somewhere in Hawaii drinking spiked pineapple juice and doing the hula.

The wolf camped permanently on our front doorstep, and his whole damn family at the back.

Days I wrote, nights I watched Ed McMahon laugh hysterically at Johnny Carson's every twitch.

I wrote another book but had no idea where to send it. The landlord had taken to coming by and yelling in a loud voice that he hadn't taken me to raise. He damn near scared the wolf off a time or two.

Then one day as I was desperately haunting the library, wondering how writers got their books in such places, the librarian asked me, "Robbie, have you ever seen a *Writer's Market?*"

That was nearly twenty years ago. The book I wrote sold to Doubleday. I couldn't believe the $1,000 advance I held in my hot little hand, and I strutted and bragged, boasted! Crowed! I was a writer!

It was two years after acceptance that *Me and Jim Luke* was published.

In the meantime, I had decided I'd best drag out the old cotton sack again. But when I opened that box from Doubleday, smelled the new ink, saw the cover—*Me and Jim Luke,* by Robbie Branscum, my mind flew back to the Arkansas hills and the three orange crates of books, and I knew that the real gold was the satisfaction of creating something from inside myself that would give others enjoyment.

A few years later, I wrote a book called *To the Tune of a Hickory Stick* about that small one-room school and its three orange crates of books, and I love to think that someday, somewhere, someplace, someone will dig through a crate of books and find one of mine. And I even dare to hope that they will feel they have found a bit of gold of their own.

One Unforgettable Acceptance Check

by Winfred Van Atta

Winfred Van Atta has been contributing to Writer's Digest *for so long that we call him "Uncle Van." Our affection for him is the same as his affection for the reader when he sits down to write. I once told him that I'd be willing to pay him ten cents a word for his letters—I find his writing that warm, and readable, and gentle.*

Gentle is a key word there. Let me point out one example: when reading this reminiscence, note that Uncle Van doesn't have to explain who Frieda is. The construction of the tale tells you. It's an unobtrusive technique he uses to communicate the relationships of people—and, yes, a gentle one.

But please save further analysis of this piece for a second reading. Devote the first reading to enjoying it.

Fifteen months after losing our first baby, Frieda and I were overwhelmed with joy when Dr. Fitzgerald informed us that Frieda was again pregnant. Blue Cross-Blue Shield was not a common fringe benefit in those early war years, so we had paid most of the doctor's fee and saved the hospital's estimated costs of $400 by the end of the seventh month.

I was then administrative assistant to Mr. Klinker, who was always offended when new acquaintances mistakenly called him Mr. Cinder. On a Saturday in late April, he invited me to accompany him to the races at Sportsman's Park, not far from our Chicago plant. I called Frieda, explaining that much as I regretted this extra chore, I'd better go because he was insistent and my raise was due in July. Frieda informed me that our old refrigerator had conked out again and Mr. Andersen had made a final negative diagnosis. However, he had one good repossessed Frigidaire in his store that we could have for $200. No new ones would be available until after the war, and what did I think? I told her to grab it and pay for it out of the baby money.

At Sportsman's Park, I lost the last of my pocket money on a horse that Mr. Klinker had assured me couldn't lose. When I asked to borrow enough for cab fare to the El, he handed me $20 and told me to get even on another sure thing in the fifth race. When he dropped me off at our building, I owed him $110.

Frieda was upset by my confession, but agreed that I should repay Mr. Klinker at once out of the baby money. I was then selling my short stories and confession pieces fairly often and I assured her that I would get the lost money back in time. To prove my sincerity, I worked most of that night to finish a short-short true story that I sent to the Chicago Daily News Syndicate. It was returned three days later with a note from the editor: "Your 'I Like to Remember George Sexton' piece is good, but you must have learned by now that we never use nonfiction. Why don't you try it with *Reader's Digest?*"

I addressed an envelope and sent the manuscript to *Reader's Digest* without an accompanying letter, then began burning the midnight oil, my panic-induced adrenaline free flowing. During the next two weeks I mailed stories to Street & Smith's *Love Story* and *Detective Story* magazines, and sent a long confession to *True Story*, feeling confident, knowing I had done my best. If they failed, we could go to those friendly people at Household Finance, who had helped us liquidate medical bills for our dear little Susan.

Saturday, June 17, 1944, had been hot and humid, and our top-floor flat on the South Side was like an oven. Frieda was uncomfortable and restless. My stories to Street & Smith and *True Story* had been returned on Friday. I was very depressed.

At 3 A.M., Frieda asked if we could move to our back porch, where a breeze was coming in off Lake Michigan. Sitting on a porch chair, Frieda suddenly gasped, then groaned. Our baby was coming two weeks early. I called a cab, found Frieda's packed bag, and rushed her up the Outer Drive to Illinois Central Hospital. The maternity unit was in an uproar when we arrived, with only one tough, elderly nurse tending three occupied labor rooms. Frieda was placed on a bed in the corridor, and I was to take care of her, by God, and stop acting like a helpless expectant father. Dr. Fitzgerald was at his summer place on a lake in Wisconsin, but his standby would be along in plenty of time. Within twenty minutes, Frieda's pains were almost constant. I'd worked in hospitals too long not to know what was about to happen.

I caught Mrs. Callahan's arm as she was galloping between labor rooms and literally dragged her bedside to Frieda. She felt once, nodded her forgiveness, and wheeled Frieda into an empty delivery room. The intern delivered Mary within minutes, it seemed, and came out to tell me we had a beautiful, perfect little girl. Frieda was being packed and I was told I should go down to the solarium and wait until the nurse called me. There, relieved and relaxed, I went to sleep on a sofa and didn't awaken until 10. The new nurse took me to see our very red, beautiful baby through the nursery window, but Frieda was sleeping and I was told I should go home and return in the afternoon.

There were no cabs around that rainy Sunday morning and the trains were running far apart, so I walked the forty blocks home through the drizzle, feeling relief and joy, but I knew that I would have to visit the finance company early Monday morning. As I came into the vestibule of our building, I remembered that I hadn't picked up Saturday's mail. Mail is never important to a writer with no stories out.

Our box contained two pale blue envelopes, each bearing the red *Reader's Digest* logo. I was quivering as I took the steps two at a time to our flat. I had completely forgotten about sending a story to *Reader's Digest*. The first letter was from Burt McBride, senior editor, who informed me that they all liked my "George Sexton" story, which would appear as a Drama in Everyday Life in an early issue. Their check for $1,500 would be along shortly from the finance office. The second letter contained the check. Later, when I was transferred to New York and had lunch with Burt McBride, I learned that his secretary had been ill and had delayed getting his acceptance letter out.

I sat down and stared at the letters and check, still trembling, still unsure that I was not experiencing another of those wish-fulfilling dreams common to beginning writers. A dollar a word seemed too fantastic to be real. I made my breakfast, then called my parents and Frieda's parents to tell them our good news, took a little bourbon to calm my nerves, and returned to the hospital, feeling guilty, as most young writers do when they write about real people, using real names. Would George, Rocky, and Mr. Klinker be offended by what I'd written about them?

George Sexton had started as mail boy at our plant, going to school nights, working his way up to head accountant. I had described him as: "One of those lonely, elderly bachelors who live quietly in YMCA hotels and wait for old age." He had taken me under his wing when I first went with Mr. Klinker, counseling me about how to work with him, and helped me get a room near his double-room corner unit at the Sears Roebuck YMCA. I would be afraid to even offer such a story to an editor today. The editor and his readers would assume that George had an unwholesome interest in young men. George was normal in every way, gentle and caring, a victim of circumstance. His father had died when George was in his late teens, leaving his mother and two young sisters without funds. George and his grandparents had kept the family together. George had put his two sisters through college and had taken care of his ill mother until her death, then moved to the Y. There wasn't a kid living there who couldn't confidently go to George for a loan between paydays. His one passion was fishing.

In late fall, George and Klinker decided to go fishing for walleye pike in Leech Lake, just out of Walker, Minnesota. I was invited to come along. We rented our cottage from sixteen-year-old Rocky Blakeman, a handsome, self-confident kid, who had built the cottage with his own hands out of logs he had cut and trimmed. His mother had died the year before, and he now lived alone, sometimes snowshoeing three miles to high school during the long winters. We were all taken with Rocky, whose knowledge of fishing, hunting, and trapping was revealed without bragging. Someday he would have many cabins and guests like us to whom he would serve as guide.

The story, as I presented it, was simple and honest, with a true-life "switch" that I had used in *Daily News* fiction plots. Sitting in a boat on Leech Lake, Klinker and I listened to George sell the boy on coming back to Chicago with him to live in a room at the Y and go to school at nearby John Marshall High School. He could work summers as mail boy at our plant, then go on to a local university when ready. Rocky came home with us, and George had found a surrogate son. Two months later, we sat in Mr. Klinker's boat near Navy Pier, fishing for Lake Michigan perch, and listened to Rocky sell George on going home with him to Leech Lake, where the air was clean and pure, the woods frosty and full of deer, with the best ice fishing in the world. George went with him and helped him establish a hunting-fishing lodge that Klinker and I visited during the several years that George was living. Rocky named his first son after George.

The new floor nurse must have read something in my face when I came onto the floor without a special admission slip. She took me to see Frieda at once.

Frieda was awake when I entered her room, wearing an expression of total joy as she pulled the blanket back to show Daddy how well our little Mary was nursing.

"And look what I found in our mailbox when I got home this morning," I said, laying the check on top of Mary's blanket.

Tears came to Frieda's eyes and she puckered her lips for me to kiss her. Just before contact, she coughed unexpectedly, her breath heavy with the odor of paraldehyde, which had been given to her as a sedative before delivery. I had given quarts of it to disturbed mental patients in restraint, who occasionally blew it back in my face when the pitcher slipped. As with ether, once sensitized to it you will always react violently each time you smell it. I burped all over that beautiful baby, mother, and check.

The nurse was not pleased with Daddy when she came to clean up the mess, but she was forgiving after learning the events that had precipitated it. As I passed her in the corridor an hour later on my way to the elevator, she smiled and said, "Happy Father's Day, Mr. Van Atta, and I'll watch for your story in *Reader's Digest*."

Yes, it was June 18, 1944, Father's Day. And if any guilt-ridden father and writer has ever received two more memorable gifts on this special day for Daddy, I've yet to meet him.

section ten

202

"RESEARCHING THE UNKNOWN"

The Final Discovery: Of the Writer Within, of the Individual Within

Back in 1971, Alex Haley wrote a piece explaining how be became fascinated with the stories his grandmother would tell about his ancestors, and then giving tips on the subject of research.

To learn about Haley's research tips, you'll have to go back to Writer's Yearbook 1972 *and read the entire text of the article. What you're about to read is just a portion of the article, the essential portion.*

Alex Haley became a rich man writing and selling the book that resulted from his research. He earned millions. He made a few bucks, too. You see, the rich-

203

es, the millions aren't to be counted in dollars, as you'll discover at the conclusion of his description of the roots of Roots.

Researching the Unknown
by Alex Haley

My Grandma Cynthia Murray Palmer lived in Henning, Tennessee (pop. 500), about fifty miles north of Memphis. As I grew up there, each summer we would be visited by several women relatives who were mostly around Grandma's age, such as my Great Aunt Liz Murray who taught in Oklahoma, and Great Aunt Till Merriwether from Jackson, Tennessee, or their considerably younger niece, Cousin Georgia Anderson from Kansas City, Kansas, and some others. Always after the supper dishes had been washed, they would go out to take seats and talk in the rocking chairs on the front porch, and I would scrounch down, listening, behind Grandma's squeaky chair, with the dusk deepening into night, and the lightning bugs flicking on and off above the now shadowy honeysuckles. What they most often talked about was the story of our family, which had been passed down for generations, until there would finally come our bedtime signal, which was the whistling blur of lights of the southbound Panama Limited train whooshing at 9:05 P.M. through Henning.

So much of their talking of people, places, and events I didn't understand. For instance, what was an "Ol' Massa," an "Ol' Missus," or a "plantation"? But early, I gathered that white folks had done lots of bad things to our folks, though I couldn't figure out why.

The furtherest-back person Grandma and the others ever talked of—always in tones of awe, I noticed—they would call "The African." They said that some ship brought him to somewhere that they pronounced " 'Naplis." They said that then some "Mas' John Waller" bought him for his plantation in "Spotsylvania County, Virginia." This African kept on escaping, the fourth time trying to kill the "hateful po' cracker" slave-catcher, who gave him the punishment choice of castration or of losing one foot. This African took a foot being chopped off with an ax against a tree stump, they said, and he was about to die. But his life was saved by "Mas' John's brother."

Crippling about, working in "Mas' William's" house and

yard, in time the African met and mated with "the big house cook named Bell," and there was born a girl named "Kizzy." She grew up with her African daddy often showing her different kinds of things, and telling her what they were—in his native tongue. Pointing at a banjo, the African uttered "ko," as example, or "Kamby Bolong," pointing at a river near the plantation. Many of his strange sounds started with a *k* sound, and the little, growing Kizzy learned gradually that they identified different things.

When addressed by other slaves as "Toby," the master's name for him, the African said angrily that his name was "Kin-tay." And as gradually *he* learned more words, of English, he told young Kizzy some things about himself—for instance that he was not far from his village, chopping wood to make himself a drum, when four men had surprised, overwhelmed, and kidnapped him.

So Kizzy's head held much about her African daddy when, at age sixteen, she was sold away, onto a much smaller plantation in North Carolina. Her new "Mas' Tom Lea" fathered her first child, a boy she named George. And Kizzy told all about his African grandfather to her boy, who grew up into such a gamecock fighter that he was called "Chicken George," and people would come from all over and "bet big money" on his cockfights. He mated with Matilda, they had seven children, and he told them the stories and strange sounds of an African great-grandfather. And one of those children, Tom, became a blacksmith, who was bought away by a "Mas' Murray," for his tobacco plantation in Alamance County, North Carolina.

Tom mated there with Irene, a weaver on the plantation. She also bore seven children, whom Tom now told all about their African great-great grandfather—the faithfully passed-down knowledge of his sounds and stories having become by now the family's prideful treasure.

The youngest of that second set of seven children was a girl, Cynthia—who became my maternal Grandma. Anyway, all of this is how I was growing up in Henning at Grandma's, listening from behind her rocking chair as she and the other visiting old women talked of that African (never then comprehended as *my* great-great-great-great grandfather) who said his name was "Kin-tay," and "ko" for banjo, "Kamby Bolong" for river, and a jumble of more *k*-beginning sounds that Grandma most often privately muttered while making beds or cooking, and that near his village he was kidnapped while chopping wood to make him a drum.

The story had become probably somewhere nearly as fixed in

my head as in Grandma's by when Dad and Mama moved me and my two younger brothers, George and Julius, away from Henning, to be with them at the small black college in Alabama where Dad taught agriculture. And compressing my next twenty-five years: more than studying in school, I "daydreamed," my parents said, preferring the vicarious reading of thrilling adventure books. Then when I was seventeen, Dad let me enlist as a messboy in the U.S. Coast Guard. Becoming a ship's cook out in the South Pacific during World War II, at nights down by my bunk I began trying to write sea adventure stories, mailing them off to magazines, and collecting rejection slips for eight years before some editors began purchasing and publishing occasional stories. By 1949, the Coast Guard made me its first "journalist"; finally with twenty years' service, I retired at thirty-seven as a Chief Journalist, determined now to make a new career of full-time writing. After a while of floundering, I wrote mostly on assignments for the *Reader's Digest;* then for *Playboy* I happened to start their "Interviews" feature, my successive subjects being controversial personages, one among them the late Malcolm X. Then, my first book attempt took a full year of really exhaustively interviewing him, and another year of writing, in the first person, as if he did, *The Autobiography of Malcolm X.*

In Washington, D.C., one Saturday in 1965, I just happened to be walking past the U.S. Archives. Across the interim years, I had thought often of Grandma's old stories—I can't reason otherwise what diverted me up the Archives' steps. And when a main reading room desk attendant asked could he help me, I wouldn't have dreamed of admitting to him some curiosity hanging on from boyhood about slave forebears I'd then heard of. I kind of bumbled that I was interested in census records of Alamance County, North Carolina, just after the Civil War.

The microfilm rolls that were delivered I kept turning through the machine, and with a building intrigue—viewing in different census-takers' vintage penmanship what seemed an endless parade of the names of people, then as living and walking around as anyone on earth, but who one day were gone forever. But after microfilmed roll after roll of it, I was beginning to tire when, in utter astonishment—I looked upon the names of *Grandma's* parents. Tom Murray, Irene Murray . . . older sisters of Grandma's, as well—Grandma wasn't even *born* yet . . . names, every one of them, that I'd heard countless times on her front porch.

It wasn't that I hadn't believed Grandma. You just *didn't* not believe my Grandma. It was simply so uncanny, the actually seeing those names in print . . . moreover, in some official U.S. Government records.

Across the next several months, whenever possible I was back in Washington, searching, in the Archives, the Library of Congress, the Daughters of the American Revolution Library.

In one source or another, in 1966 I was able to document at least the highlights of the cherished family story. I would have given anything to tell Grandma, but sadly in 1949 she had gone. So I went and told the only survivor of those Henning front-porch storytellers, Cousin Georgia Anderson, now in her eighties in Kansas City, Kansas. Wrinkled, bent, not well herself, she was *so* overjoyed, repeating to me the old stories and sounds; they were like Henning echoes: "Yeah, boy, that African say his name was 'Kin-tay'; he say the banjo was 'ko,' an' the river 'Kamby-Bolong,' an' he was off choppin' some wood to make his drum, when they grabbed 'im!" Cousin Georgia grew so excited we had to stop her, to calm her down. "You go 'head, boy! Your grandma an' all of 'em—they up there watchin' what you do!"

Those strange, unknown-tongue sounds, always part of our family's old story . . . they were obviously bits of our original African "Kin-tay's" native tongue. What specific tongue? Could I somehow find out?

In New York, I began making visits to the United Nations Headquarters' lobby; it wasn't hard to spot Africans. I'd stop any I could, asking if my bits of phonetic sounds held for them any meaning. A couple of dozen Africans quickly looked at me, listened, and took off—understandably, from some Tennesseean's accent alleging "African" sounds.

An expert researcher friend, George Sims (we grew up together in Henning), brought me some names of ranking scholars of African linguistics. Particularly intriguing was one, a Belgian- and English-educated Dr. Jan Vansina; he had spent his early career living in West African villages, studying and tape recording countless of the oral histories that were narrated by certain very old African men.

So I flew to the University of Wisconsin where Dr. Vansina was. In his living room, I told him every bit of the family story, to the fullest detail I could remember it. Then, intensely, he queried me, about the story's physical relay across the generations, about the kind of gibberish of *k* sounds that sometimes Grandma had fiercely muttered to herself while doing her housework, with my brothers and me giggling beyond her hearing at what we dubbed "Grandma's noises."

Dr. Vansina finally said, his manner very serious, "These sounds your family has kept sound very probably of the tongue called 'Mandinka.' "

I'd never heard of any "Mandinka." Grandma just told of the African saying such as "ko" for banjo, or "Kamby Bolong" for a Virginia river.

Among Mandinka stringed instruments, Dr. Vansina said, one of the oldest was the "kora."

"Bolong," he said was clearly Mandinka for "river." Preceded by "Kamby," very likely it meant "Gambia River."

Dr. Vansina telephoned an eminent Africanist colleague, Dr. Philip Curtin. He said that the phonetic *Kin-tay* was correctly spelled *Kinte*, a very old clan that had originated in Old Mali. The Kinte men traditionally were blacksmiths, and the women were potters and weavers.

I knew I must get to the Gambia River.

The first native Gambian I could locate in the U.S. was named Ebou Manga, then a junior attending Hamilton College in upstate Clinton, New York. He and I flew on Pan American to Dakar, Senegal, thence took a smaller plane to Yundum Airport, and rode in a van to The Gambia's capital, Bathurst. Ebou and his father assembled eight Gambian government members. I told them Grandma's stories, every detail I could remember, as they listened intently, then reacted. " 'Kamby Bolong' of course is Gambia River!" I heard. "But more clue is your forefather's saying his name was 'Kinte.' " Then they told me something I never would have even fantasized— that in places in the back country lived very old men, commonly called *griots*, who could tell centuries of the histories of certain very old family clans. As for Kintes, they pointed out to me on a map even some family villages, Kinte-Kundah, Kinte-Kundah Janneh-Ya, for instance.

The Gambian government members said they would make efforts to aid me. I returned to New York dazed. It is embarrassing to me now, but only to tell the truth: despite Grandma's stories, I'd never been concerned much regarding Africa, beyond its location on world maps, and I held the routine illusions of African people mostly among exotic jungles. But such a compulsion now laid hold of me to learn all I could that I began devouring books about Africa, especially circa the slave trade. Then one Thursday's mail contained a letter from one of the Gambian officials, inviting my return there.

Monday I was back in Bathurst. It simply galvanized me when the officials said that a *griot* was located who told the Kinte clan history—his name was Kebba Kanga Fofana. To reach him, I discovered, required a modified safari, renting a launch to get up river, two land vehicles to carry supplies by a roundabout, longer land route, and employing finally fourteen people, including three interpreters and four musicians, as a *griot* would not speak the reversed clan histories without background music.

The boat *Baddibu* vibrated upriver, with me acutely tense: were these Africans maybe viewing me as but another of the pith-helmets? After about two hours, we put in at James Island, for me to see the ruins of once British-operated James Fort, where two centuries of slaveships had loaded thousands of cargoes of Gambian tribespeople. The crumbling stones, the deeply oxidized swivel cannon, even still some remnant links of chains, seemed all but impossible to believe—but there they were to gaze at. Then we continued upriver to the left-bank village of Albreda, and there put ashore, now to continue on foot to the Juffure village of the griot. Once more we stopped, for me to see *Toubob kolong,* meaning "The white man's well," now almost filled in, and in swampy surrounding area, with abounding tall, saw-toothed grass, a century since it was dug to "seventeen men's height deep," to ensure survival drinking water for long-driven, famishing coffles of slaves recently taken.

Walking on, I kept wishing that Grandma could hear how her stories had led me to the "Kamby Bolong." (Our surviving storyteller Cousin Georgia died in a Kansas City hospital during this morning, I would learn later.) Finally, Juffure village's playing children, sighting us, flashed an alert. The seventy-odd people came rushing from their circular, thatch-roofed, mud-walled huts, with goats bounding up and about, and parrots squawking from up in the palms. I sensed him in advance somehow, the small man amid them, wearing a pillbox cap and an off-white robe—the *griot.* Then the interpreters did go to him, as the villagers thronged around me.

And it hit me like a gale wind: every one of them, the whole crowd, was *jet black.* A sense of some enormous *guilt* swept me . . . sense of being some kind of a *hybrid*—sense of being impure, among *pure.* It was a very awful sensation.

The old *griot,* stepping away from my interpreters, quickly was swarmed around by the crowd—all of them buzzing. An interpreter named A. B. C. Salla came to me; he whispered: "Why they stare at you so, they have never seen here a black American."

The impact of that hit me: I was symbolizing for them twenty-five millions of us they had never seen. What did they think of me—of us?

Then abruptly the old *griot* was briskly walking toward me.

His eyes boring into mine, he spoke in Mandinka, as if instinctively I should understand—and A. B. C. Salla translated:

"Yes . . . we have been told by the forefathers . . . that many of us from this place are in exile . . . in that place called America . . . and in other places."

I suppose I physically wavered, and they thought it was the heat; rustling whispers went through the crowd, and a man brought me a low stool. Now, the whispering hushed—the musicians had softly begun playing *kora* and *balafon,* and a canvas sling lawn seat was being taken by the *griot,* Kebba Kanga Fofana, age seventy three "rains" (one rainy season each year). He seemed as if gathering himself into a physical rigidity. And he began speaking the Kinte clan's ancestral oral history; it came rolling from his mouth across the next hours . . . seventeenth- and into eighteenth-century Kinte lineage details, predominantly what men took what wives; the children they "begot," in the order of their births; those children's mates and children. *When* things had taken place frequently was dated by some proximate singular physical occurrence. It was as if indelible within the *griot's* brain was some ancient scroll. Each few sentences or so, he would pause for an interpreter's translation to me. I distill here to a lineal very essence:

The Kinte clan began in Old Mali, the men generally blacksmiths "who conquered fire," and the women were potters and weavers. One large branch of the clan moved into Mauretania . . . from where one son of the clan, Kairaba Kunta Kinte, a Moslem marabout holy man, entered The Gambia. He lived first in the village of Pakali N'Ding; he moved next to Jiffarong village; "and then he came here, into our own village of Juffure."

In Juffure, Kairaba Kunta Kinte took his first wife, "a Mandinka maiden, whose name was Sireng. By her, he begot two sons, whose names were Janneh and Saloum. Then he got a second wife, Yaisa. By her, he begot a son, Omoro."

The three sons became men in Juffure. Janneh and Saloum went off and founded a new village, Kinte-Kundah Janneh-Ya. "And then Omoro, the youngest son, when he had thirty rains, took as a wife a maiden, Binta Kebba.

"And by her, he begot four sons—Kunta, Lamin, Suwadu, and Madi . . ."

Sometimes, a "begotten," after their naming, would be accompanied by some later-occurring detail, perhaps as "in time of big water [flood], he slew a water buffalo." Having named those four sons, now the *griot* stated such a detail.

"About the time the king's soldiers came, the eldest of these four sons, Kunta, when he had about sixteen rains, went away from this village, to chop wood to make a drum . . . and he was never seen again—"

Goose pimples the size of lemons seemed popping over me. In my knapsack were my cumulative notebooks, the first of them including how in my boyhood, my Grandma, Cousin Georgia, and the others told of the African "Kin-tay" who always said he was kidnapped near his village—while chopping wood to make a drum . . .

Somehow, I showed the interpreter; he showed and told the *griot*, who excitedly told the people; they grew very agitated. Abruptly then they formed a human ring, encircling me, dancing and chanting. Maybe a dozen of the women carrying their infant babies rushed in toward me, thrusting forth the infants into my embracing efforts—conveying, I would later learn, "the laying on of hands . . . through this flesh which is us, we are you, and you are us." The men hurried me into their mosque, their Arabic praying later being translated outside: "Thanks be to Allah for returning the long lost from among us." Direct descendants of Kunta Kinte's blood brothers were hastened, some of them from nearby villages, for a family portrait to be taken with me . . . surrounded by actual ancestral sixth cousins.

Let me tell you something: I am a man. But I remember the surging sob from my feet, flinging up my hands before my face and bawling as not since I was a baby . . . the jet-black Africans were jostling, staring . . . I didn't care, with it surging that if you really knew the odyssey of us millions of black Americans, if you really knew how we came in the seeds of our forefathers, captured, driven, beaten, inspected, bought, branded, chained in foul ships, if you really knew, you needed weeping. . . .

Back home, I knew that what I must write, really, was our black saga, where any individual's past is the essence of the millions'.

Other Books of Interest

General Writing Books

Beginning Writer's Answer Book, edited by Kirk Polking (paper) $12.95

Getting the Words Right: How to Revise, Edit and Rewrite, by Theodore A. Rees Cheney $14.95

How to Become a Bestselling Author, by Stan Corwin $14.95

How to Get Started in Writing, by Peggy Teeters (paper) $8.95

How to Increase Your Word Power, by the editors of Reader's Digest $19.95

How to Write a Book Proposal, by Michael Larsen $9.95

How to Write While You Sleep, by Elizabeth Ross $14.95

If I Can Write, You Can Write, by Charlie Shedd $12.95

International Writers' & Artists' Yearbook (paper) $14.95

Just Open a Vein, edited by William Brohaugh $15.95

Knowing Where to Look: The Ultimate Guide to Research, by Lois Horowitz $18.95

Law & the Writer, edited by Polking & Meranus (paper) $10.95

Make Every Word Count, by Gary Provost (paper) $7.95

Pinckert's Practical Grammar, by Robert C. Pinckert $14.95

Teach Yourself to Write, by Evelyn Stenbock (paper) $9.95

The 29 Most Common Writing Mistakes & How to Avoid Them, by Judy Delton $9.95

Writer's Block & How to Use It, by Victoria Nelson $14.95

The Writer's Digest Guide to Manuscript Formats, by Buchman & Groves $16.95

Writer's Encyclopedia, edited by Kirk Polking (paper) $16.95

Writer's Guide to Research, by Lois Horowitz $9.95

Writer's Market, edited by Glenda Neff $21.95

Writing for the Joy of It, by Leonard Knott $11.95

Nonfiction Writing

Basic Magazine Writing, by Barbara Kevles $16.95

How to Sell Every Magazine Article You Write, by Lisa Collier Cool $14.95

How to Write & Sell the 8 Easiest Article Types, by Helene Schellenberg Barnhart $14.95

Writing Creative Nonfiction, by Theodore A. Rees Cheney $15.95

Writing Nonfiction that Sells, by Samm Sinclair Baker $14.95

Fiction Writing

Creating Short Fiction, by Damon Knight (paper) $8.95

Fiction is Folks: How to Create Unforgettable Characters, by Robert Newton Peck (paper) $8.95

Fiction Writer's Help Book, by Maxine Rock $12.95

Fiction Writer's Market, edited by Laurie Henry $18.95

Handbook of Short Story Writing, by Dickson and Smythe (paper) $8.95

How to Write & Sell Your First Novel, by Oscar Collier with Frances Spatz Leighton $14.95

How to Write Short Stories that Sell, by Louise Boggess (paper) $7.95

One Way to Write Your Novel, by Dick Perry (paper) $7.95

Storycrafting, by Paul Darcy Boles (paper) $9.95

Writing the Novel: From Plot to Print, by Lawrence Block (paper) $8.95

Special Interest Writing Books

The Children's Picture Book: How to Write It, How to Sell It, by Ellen E.M. Roberts (paper) $14.95

Comedy Writing Secrets, by Melvin Helitzer $16.95

The Complete Book of Scriptwriting, by J. Michael Straczynski (paper) $9.95

The Complete Guide to Writing Software User Manuals, by Brad M. McGehee (paper) $14.95

How to Make Money Writing Fillers, by Connie Emerson (paper) $8.95
How to Sell & Re-Sell Your Writing, by Duane Newcomb $10.95
How to Write a Cookbook and Get It Published, by Sara Pitzer $15.95
How to Write & Sell A Column, by Raskin & Males $10.95
How to Write and Sell Your Personal Experiences, by Lois Duncan (paper) $9.95
How to Write and Sell (Your Sense of) Humor, by Gene Perret (paper) $9.95
How to Write Tales of Horror, Fantasy & Science Fiction, edited by J.N. Williamson $15.95
How to Write the Story of Your Life, by Frank P. Thomas $14.95
How You Can Make $50,000 a Year as a Nature Photojournalist, by Bill Thomas (paper) $17.95
Mystery Writer's Handbook, by The Mystery Writers of America (paper) $9.95
Nonfiction for Children: How to Write It, How to Sell It, by Ellen E.M. Roberts $16.95
On Being a Poet, by Judson Jerome $14.95
The Poet's Handbook, by Judson Jerome (paper) $8.95
Poet's Market, by Judson Jerome $17.95
Successful Outdoor Writing, by Jack Samson $11.95
Travel Writer's Handbook, by Louise Zobel (paper) $10.95
TV Scriptwriter's Handbook, by Alfred Brenner (paper) $9.95
Writing After 50, by Leonard L. Knott $12.95
Writing for Children & Teenagers, by Lee Wyndham (paper) $9.95
Writing for the Soaps, by Jean Rouverol $14.95
Writing Short Stories for Young People, by George Edward Stanley $15.95
Writing the Modern Mystery, by Barbara Norville $15.95

The Writing Business
A Beginner's Guide to Getting Published, edited by Kirk Polking $10.95
Complete Guide to Self-Publishing, by Tom & Marilyn Ross $19.95
Editing for Print, by Geoffrey Rogers $14.95
Freelance Jobs for Writers, edited by Kirk Polking (paper) $8.95
How to Bulletproof Your Manuscript, by Bruce Henderson $9.95
How to Get Your Book Published, by Herbert W. Bell $15.95
How to Understand and Negotiate a Book Contract or Magazine Agreement, by Richard Balkin $11.95
How to Write Irresistible Query Letters, by Lisa Collier Cool $10.95
How You Can Make $25,000 a Year Writing (No Matter Where You Live), by Nancy Edmonds Hanson $15.95
Literary Agents: How to Get & Work with the Right One for You, by Michael Larsen $9.95
Professional Etiquette for Writers, by William Brohaugh $9.95

To order directly from the publisher, include $2.00 postage and handling for 1 book and 50¢ for each additional book. Allow 30 days for delivery.

Writer's Digest Books, Department B
1507 Dana Avenue, Cincinnati, Ohio 45207
Credit card orders call TOLL-FREE
1-800-543-4644 (Outside Ohio)
1-800-551-0884 (Ohio only)
Prices subject to change without notice.

For information on how to receive Writer's Digest Books at special Book Club member prices, please write to:

Promotion Manager
Writer's Digest Book Club
1507 Dana Avenue
Cincinnati, Ohio 45207